英語で読む
グリム名作選
The Best of Grimm's Fairy Tales

グリム兄弟
原作

出水田隆文
英語解説

宇野葉子
翻訳

カバーイラスト
John Bauer
•
本文イラスト
Otto Ubbelohde, Alexander Zick (p.111)
•
英文リライト
Ron Davidson
•
ナレーション
J. King, Melinda Joe

本書の英語テキストは、弊社から刊行された
ラダーシリーズ『The Best of Grimm's Fairy Tales グリム名作選』から転載しています。

はじめに

　グリム童話は「聖書に継ぐベストセラー」とも言われています。世代を超えて子供たちを楽しませ、その想像力を豊かにしてきただけでなく、芸術や文学をはじめ様々な分野にクリエイティブな影響を及ぼしています。

　誰もが知る「グリム童話」ですが、グリム兄弟がどのような人物だったのか、なぜ童話を収集・編纂したのかを知る人は少ないことでしょう。グリム童話が成立した背景を知っておくと、物語をより一層楽しむことができます。

グリム兄弟って誰？

　グリム童話集を作ったグリム兄弟とは、兄のJacob Grimm（1785-1863）と弟のWilhelm Grimm（1786-1859）の二人のことです。ドイツ語読みでヤーコプとヴィルヘルムと読みます。この二人に加えて、挿絵などを担当した末弟のルートヴィッヒを付け加えることもあります。ちなみにグリム兄弟は男5人に女1人の6人兄弟です。2人兄弟だと思っていた読者の方も多いのではないでしょうか。

　ヤーコプとヴィルヘルムは童話作家ではない、と知ったらきっと驚かれることでしょう。実は二人は言語学者です。裕福な家に生まれた二人でしたが、父の死後一家は困窮に陥ります。貧しさに負けずに勉学を続け、二人は大学教授となりました。ドイツの古文学や民間伝承などを研究する言語学者でした。二人はなぜ童話集を作ろうとしたのでしょうか？

当時のドイツ

　グリム童話集の成り立ちを考えるためには、当時のヨーロッパ情勢を知っておく必要があります。当時のドイツは、と言っても、当時ドイツという国家は存在しませんでした。17世紀以降、今のドイツの場所にはおよそ300もの領邦と呼ばれる独立国が存在していました。隣国のフランスが絶対王政の元、中央集権化を図り国力を蓄えたのとは対照的に、当時のドイツは国民国家としての統一が遅れていました。そのため19世紀初頭のナポレオンの侵攻に対抗することができずに、連戦連敗を喫しフランス軍に屈してしまいます。

　敗戦の屈辱を機に、ドイツで「みんなで一つにまとまろう」という機運が高まります。35の領邦と4つの自由都市が同盟を結成し「ドイツ連邦」が1815年に結成されます。その後の変遷を経て1871年にようやく「ドイツ統一」がなされました。まさにそのような時代背景のなか、1812年にグリム童話集第1版は刊行されました。グリム童話集の正式名称は「子供たちと家庭の童話」（原題Kinder- und Hausmärchen）です。

グリム兄弟がグリム童話に込めた想い

　グリム兄弟はドイツ語を研究し、体系的にまとめることに情熱を傾けました。その研究の一つとして各地に伝わる民話や伝承を集め発表することで、ドイツ語を話す人々がまとまるきっかけの一つになってほしいと考えていたようです。同じ言語を共有していることを人々が実感し、「ああ、この話って僕らの国でも昔から人気だよね！　僕らはルーツが同じだね！」となることを期待したのでしょう。

言語で人々を一つにしようと願っていたグリム兄弟が、インターネットと英語をベースに、急速にグローバル化が進む現代の世界を見たらどのような感想を持つのか聞いてみたいものですね。

　グリム兄弟は、ドイツ各地の口承・伝承を聞き取り調査し、民話を収集しました。一部は他国の伝承と類似したものもあるのですが、国と国が地続きのヨーロッパですから口承が国を超えて伝わるのは当然といえば当然です。

　初版と第2版は口承そのままの文章で飾り気がなく、私たちが現在目にする童話の形とは程遠く、たんなる民話の記録集でした。「子供たちと家庭の童話」というタイトルの割には、まだ児童向けといえる本ではなかったようです。

　本として商業的に成功を収めるようになったのは、挿絵をいれ物語を脚色し、エンターテイメント性を高めた第3版以降でした。

　弟のヴィルヘルムが、主に物語性を高めるための脚色、残虐な場面や性的な表現の変更など、童話にふさわしいものにするための改訂に取り組みました。末弟のルートヴィッヒも挿絵を担当し、改訂に携わったことは先に述べたとおりです。グリム童話は1812年の初版から、1857年の第7版まで改訂を重ねます。第7版では200編もの物語が収録されました。

　兄のヤーコプはあまりそのような改訂には興味を持っていなかったようです。言語学者・古文学者として、またドイツナショナリズムに貢献する者として、民話を集め発表したことで当初の目的を達したと思っていたのかもしれません。

　しかし、ヤーコプの情熱が失われていたわけではありません。ヤーコプはゲルマン古典文献学・ゲルマン語学・ドイツ文献学の基礎を築いたと言われています。ドイツ語の言語研究はヤーコプ（もちろんヴィルヘル

ムも）なしでは語ることはできないのです。

　弟ヴィルヘルムとの共同編著「ドイツ語辞典」は、彼の死後およそ100年経って、ようやく完成したほどの大作です。著書「ドイツ文法」の中で、後に「グリムの法則」と呼ばれることになる音韻の法則を発表し、ヨーロッパの比較言語学の礎ともなりました。他にも彼の研究の成果のいくつかが、現代の比較神話学や民俗学へと発展したことも忘れてはいけません。

　グリム童話はグリム兄弟の言語学・古文学研究の産物です。二人の「祖国の言葉」を愛する一途な探究心と、「言葉で人々を一つにしたい」という崇高な理念がその根底にはあるのです。

現代のグリム童話

　グリム童話は、絵本やアニメなど様々な形で、世界中で親しまれています。民話や童話の常ではありますが、国や文化に応じて様々な変更が加えられて、同じ物語でも多種多様なバリエーションが存在しています。またグリム童話集をきっかけに世界各国で民話収集・研究が盛んになりました。

　本場ドイツではグリム兄弟の出身地ハーナウから「ブレーメンの音楽隊」の舞台ブレーメンまでの600kmの街道が「ドイツメルヘン街道」として整備され、観光にも一役買っています。街道沿いにはメルヘン発祥の街が多数あり、世界中から訪れるファンが童話の舞台を楽しんでいます。

最後に

　グリム童話には『ヘンゼルとグレーテル』『シンデレラ』『赤ずきんちゃん』『白雪姫』『ねむり姫』など誰もが知る物語も含めて、実は200編もの物語が収められています。本書では、グリム兄弟の情熱によって編纂されたこの素晴らしい童話集の中から、英語の学習にぴったりの物語を8編選びました。

　牧歌的でありながらも、どこか滑稽で哀愁を感じさせる童話の数々は、語り継いできたドイツの人々の息づかいまでも現代に伝えているかのようです。

　グリム兄弟の情熱とドイツの人々の暮らしと歴史に思いを馳せながら、英語でグリム童話を味わいましょう！ようこそメルヘンの世界へ！

本書の構成

本書は、

　　　□ 英日対訳による本文　　　□ 欄外の語注
　　　□ 覚えておきたい英語表現　□ MP3形式の英文音声

で構成されています。

　本書は、「グリム童話」をやさしい英語で書きあらためた本文に、日本語訳をつけました。

　各ページの下部には、英語を読み進める上で助けとなるよう単語・熟語の意味が掲載されています。また左右ページは、段落のはじまりが対応していますので、日本語を読んで英語を確認するという読み方もスムーズにできるようになっています。またシーンごとに英語解説がありますので、本文を楽しんだ後に、英語の使い方などをチェックしていただくのに最適です。

付属のCD-ROMについて

本書に付属のCD-ROMに収録されている音声は、パソコンや携帯音楽プレーヤーなどで再生することができるMP3ファイル形式です。一般的な音楽CDプレーヤーでは再生できませんので、ご注意ください。

■音声ファイルについて

　付属のCD-ROMには、本書の英語パートの朗読音声が収録されています。本文左ページに出てくるヘッドホンマーク内の数字とファイル名の数字がそれぞれ対応しています。

　パソコンや携帯プレーヤーで、お好きな箇所を繰り返し聴いていただくことで、発音のチェックだけでなく、英語で物語を理解する力が自然に身に付きます。

■音声ファイルの利用方法について

　CD-ROMをパソコンのCD/DVDドライブに入れて、iTunesやx-アプリなどの音楽再生(管理)ソフトにCD-ROM上の音声ファイルを取り込んでご利用ください。

■パソコンの音楽再生ソフトへの取り込みについて

　パソコンにMP3形式の音声ファイルを再生できるアプリケーションがインストールされていることをご確認ください。

　通常のオーディオCDと異なり、CD-ROMをパソコンのCD/DVDドライブに入れても、多くの場合音楽再生ソフトは自動的に起動しません。ご自分でアプリケーションを直接起動して、「ファイル」メニューから「ライブラリに追加」したり、再生ソフトのウインドウ上にファイルをマウスでドラッグ&ドロップするなどして取り込んでください。

　音楽再生ソフトの詳しい操作方法や、携帯音楽プレーヤーへのファイルの転送方法については、ソフトやプレーヤーに付属のマニュアルやオンラインヘルプで確認するか、アプリケーションの開発元にお問い合わせください。

CONTENTS

はじめに 3

Part 1

Hansel and Gretel *12*
ヘンゼルとグレーテル

Part 2

The Frog Prince *50*
カエルの王子

The Bottled Spirit *64*
瓶のなかのお化け

The Three Spinning Women *82*
糸を紡ぐ三人の女

Part 3

The Shoes That Were Danced Full of Holes *94*
踊ってぼろぼろになった靴

The Fisherman and His Wife *110*
漁師とおかみさん

Part 4

The Brave Little Tailor *136*
勇ましいちびの仕立て屋

The Golden Goose *166*
金のガチョウ

Part 1

Hansel and Gretel
ヘンゼルとグレーテル

 # Hansel and Gretel

Once upon a time, a poor woodcutter lived near a big woods with his wife and two children, a boy and a girl. The boy was called Hansel, and the girl, Gretel. They never had nice things to eat. Sometimes, when there was a food shortage in the land, they could not even get bread. One night, as the father lay in bed, he was very troubled.

"What will happen to us? How can we feed our little ones when we have nothing to eat ourselves?" he asked his wife.

"Listen," answered his wife, "early tomorrow morning we will take the children far into the woods, light them a fire, give each of them a piece of bread, then leave them alone. They will never find their way home and we will not have to feed them any more."

■once upon a time むかしむかし ■wood 名森 ■shortage 名不足 ■feed 動～を養う ■light a fire 火をおこす ■find one's way home 家に帰ってくる

ヘンゼルとグレーテル

　むかしむかし、大きな森のそばに、貧しい木こりがおかみさんと2人の子どもといっしょに住んでいた。男の子はヘンゼル、女の子はグレーテルといった。この一家には食べる物もろくになかった。国ではときどき飢饉が起こり、パンを手に入れることさえできなかった。ある晩、父親は寝床にいて、とても不安になった。

「わしらはどうなるんだろう？　自分たちが食べる物さえないのに、どうやって子どもたちを養ったらいいんだ？」亭主はおかみさんにたずねた。
「ねえ、聞いて」おかみさんが答えた。「明日の朝早く、子どもたちを森の奥に連れていき、たき火をしてやって、一切れずつパンをやるのさ。それから置き去りにしよう。子どもたちには家に帰る道がわかりっこないから、もう養ってやる必要がなくなるってもんだ」

Hansel and Gretel

"No, wife," said the man, "I cannot do that. I cannot leave my two little children alone in the woods. They will probably be eaten by wild animals."

"Oh!" said she, "then all four of us will die of hunger." Finally, the poor woodcutter agreed to her plan.

The two children, however, were so hungry that they couldn't sleep. They had heard their stepmother's plan. Gretel said to Hansel, "We will die, dear brother."

"Don't cry Gretel," said Hansel, "I will make sure we don't die."

When the old folks went to sleep, Hansel put on his coat and quietly went out the back door. The moon was shining brightly and the white stones on the path in front of the house shone like silver coins. Hansel filled his pockets full of stones and returned to his room.

"Don't be afraid, little sister," he said to Gretel, "God will not forget us. Now try to get some sleep."

Early the next day the woman called the two children.

■die of ～がもとで死ぬ ■hunger 名飢え ■stepmother 名継母 ■old folks 年長の家族[両親] ■path 名小道

ヘンゼルとグレーテル

「とんでもないよ、おまえ」亭主が言った。「わしにはそんなことはできない。森のなかに小さな2人の子どもたちを置き去りにするなんて、できやしない。たぶん、森のけものたちに食べられてしまうよ」

「まあ!」おかみさんが言った。「このままだと、4人とも飢え死にしてしまうじゃないか」。とうとう、貧しい木こりはおかみさんの計画に従うことになった。

ところが、2人の子どもたちはおなかが減りすぎて眠れなかったので、継母の計画を聞いてしまった。グレーテルはヘンゼルに言った。「わしたち、死んでしまうのね、兄さん」

「泣くのはおよし、グレーテル」ヘンゼルが言った。「死なないですむようにするからね」

両親が眠りにつくと、ヘンゼルは上着を着て、そっと裏口から出ていった。月がこうこうと照り、家の前の道に散らばった白い小石が銀貨のように輝いていた。ヘンゼルは小石をポケットが一杯になるまで詰め込んで、部屋に戻った。

「怖がらなくていいよ、グレーテル」兄は妹に言った。「神様はぼくたちのことを忘れたりなさらない。さあ、少し眠っておこう」

次の朝早く、おかみさんは子どもたちを起こしに来た。

Hansel and Gretel

"Get up, both of you," she said, "and come with us into the woods to gather sticks." She gave each of them a piece of bread and told them it was for dinner. She told them not to eat it because they would get nothing else.

Soon, they left together for the woods. They had not gone far when Hansel stopped. He looked back at the house. He did this again and again. His father said, "Hansel, what are you looking at?"

"Oh, father," said Hansel, "I am looking at my white dog sitting on the roof waving good-bye to me."

"That isn't your dog, you fool!" said his stepmother, "it's the morning sunlight shining on a stone." But Hansel had not really been looking at the dog; he was dropping the stones out of his pocket.

When they came to the middle of the woods the father said, "Now, children, gather sticks and we will make a fire."

■stick 図たきぎ ■nothing else 他には何もない ■wave 動手などをふって別れの挨拶をする ■you fool バカものめ ■drop 動落とす

ヘンゼルとグレーテル

「さあ、起きるんだ、おまえたち」おかみさんが言った。「わたしたちについて、森にたきぎを拾いにいくんだよ」。おかみさんは子どもたちにそれぞれパンを一切れ持たせ、昼ごはんにするように言い、すぐに食べてはいけないよ、ほかには何も食べ物がないからねと注意した。

まもなく、みんなはいっしょに森に出かけていった。しばらく行くと、ヘンゼルが立ち止まり、家を振り返った。何度も何度もそれを繰り返した。父親がたずねた。「ヘンゼル、何を見ているんだい？」

「ああ、お父さん」ヘンゼルが答えた。「ぼくの白い犬が屋根の上に座って、ぼくにさよならを言っているんだ」

「あれはおまえの犬なんかじゃないよ、ばかだねえ」継母が言った。「朝日が石にあたって光っているだけさ」。けれども、ヘンゼルは本当に犬を見ていたわけではなかった。ポケットから小石を落としていたのだった。

森のまんなかまで来ると、父親が言った。「さあ、子どもたち、たきぎを集めておいで。それで、火を起こしてあげるから」

Hansel and Gretel

　Hansel and Gretel gathered up many sticks, and when the fire was burning strongly, the woman said, "You can lie down by the fire and rest yourselves while we go further to cut wood. When we have finished we will come and get you."

　Hansel and Gretel sat by the fire. When dinner-time came, they ate their bread. They could still hear the sound of wood being cut. They thought that their father was close by. However, their father had tied a branch to a tree. Every time the wind blew, the branch hit the tree. This was the noise the children heard. They were very tired and soon they fell asleep in front of the fire. They did not wake up until it was night and very dark. Gretel began to cry, and said, "We shall never find our way out of the woods."

　"Wait," said Hansel, "the moon will be up in a minute. Then we'll find our way out quickly."

■gather up 集める　■close by すぐ近くに　■branch 名枝　■blew 動blow（風が吹く）の過去　■in a minute すぐに　■shall 助必ず~となるだろう　■way out 出口

ヘンゼルとグレーテル

　ヘンゼルとグレーテルはたきぎをたくさん集め、炎が高く燃え上がると、おかみさんが言った。「火のそばで横になって、休んでいていいよ。わたしたちはもっと奥へ行って、木を切って来るよ。それが終わったら、迎えに来るからね」

　ヘンゼルとグレーテルは火のそばに座り、昼ごはんの時間になると、めいめい自分のパンを食べた。木を切る音がまだ聞こえていたので、2人は父親がすぐ近くにいると思っていた。ところが、父親が木に結びつけておいた枝が、風が吹くたびに木にぶつかっていただけだった。子どもたちが聞いていたのは、その音だった。2人はとても疲れていたので、すぐに火の前で眠り込んだ。目を覚ますと夜になっていて、まっ暗だった。グレーテルは泣き出して言った。「森から出る道がわからないわ」

　「ちょっと待つんだよ」ヘンゼルが言った。「もうすぐお月様が出る。そしたら、すぐに道が見つかるよ」

Hansel and Gretel

Soon the great full moon rose in the sky, and Hansel took his little sister's hand and followed the stones. The stones shone brightly and showed them the way home. The children walked all night, and at dawn they reached their father's house. They knocked at the door and when the woman opened it and saw Hansel and Gretel she looked surprised. Then she quickly said, "Why did you sleep so long in the woods? We began to think you were not coming back at all."

The father was delighted to see the children. He felt that it was wrong to leave them alone and helpless.

A short time later, there was another food shortage.

The children heard their stepmother saying to their father, "There is hardly anything left to eat, only a little bread. What will we do when that is gone? We must leave the children in the forest. This time we will take them deeper into the woods, so that they will not be able to find their way out. It's the only thing we can do to save us."

■dawn 名夜明け　■not 〜 at all まったく〜しない　■be delighted to 〜して喜ぶ
■hardly anything ほとんど何もない　■so that 〜のために

ヘンゼルとグレーテル

　まもなく、大きな満月が空に昇ると、ヘンゼルは妹の手を取って、小石をたどった。小石は明るく輝き、家までの道を教えてくれた。子どもたちは夜通し歩き、夜明けになると父親の家にたどり着いた。2人が戸をたたくと、おかみさんが戸をあけ、ヘンゼルとグレーテルを見て驚いたようだった。そしてすぐに言った。「何だって、そんなに遅くまで森で寝ていたのだい？　もう帰ってこないと思っていたところだよ」

　父親は子どもたちを見て喜んだ。子どもたちを身を守ることもできないところに置き去りにしたことを後悔していたのだ。
　しばらくすると、新たな飢饉がやって来た。
　子どもたちは継母が父親に言うのを聞いた。「もうほとんど食べる物がないよ。ほんのわずかなパンだけさ。それもなくなったらどうすりゃいいの？　子どもたちを森に置いてこなくちゃならないね。今度は、森のもっと奥まで連れていって、帰る道がわからないようにしなくちゃならない。そうするより、わたしたちの助かる道はないからね」

Hansel and Gretel

The man's heart was heavy, and he thought, "I would rather share our last bread with the children." But the woman had made up her mind, and she would not listen to the man. He gave in the first time and he gave in the second time too.

The children, however, had heard everything. When his parents went to sleep, Hansel got up again to go out and pick up some stones. But, he couldn't go outside because the woman had closed the door. He said to his little sister, "Don't worry, Gretel, don't cry, go to sleep. God will take care of us."

The next morning the woman woke the children. She gave them each a piece of bread. It was a smaller piece of bread than last time.

As they walked to the woods Hansel broke the bread in his pocket and dropped little pieces on the ground.

■would rather ～するほうがいい　■make up one's mind 決心を固める　■give in 要求を受け入れる　■take care of ～を保護する　■last time この前のとき

ヘンゼルとグレーテル

　亭主の心は重く、「最後のパンを子どもたちとわかち合うほうがいい」と思った。ところが、おかみさんの決心は固く、亭主の意見にまったく耳を貸さなかった。亭主は最初にそうであったように、今度もおかみさんの言いなりになってしまった。

　ところが、子どもたちは一部始終を聞いていた。両親が眠りにつくと、ヘンゼルはまた起き上がり、外に出て小石を拾おうとした。でも、外に出ることはできなかった。おかみさんが戸に鍵をかけていたからだ。兄は妹に言った。「心配しないで、グレーテル。泣かないで、眠るんだよ。神様がお守りくださるからね」

　次の朝、おかみさんは子どもたちを起こし、パンを一切れずつわたした。パンは前のときより小さかった。

　森に向かう途中で、ヘンゼルはポケットのなかでパンを粉々にして、小さなかけらを地面に落としていった。

Hansel and Gretel

The woman led the children deeper and deeper into the forest. She led them to a part they had never been before. Again, a large fire was made and their stepmother said, "Stay here, children, and when you are tired have a sleep. We are going further to cut wood. When we have finished we will come for you."

When dinner-time came Gretel shared her bread with Hansel, because he had dropped his as they walked along. Then they fell asleep. The evening went by and no one came to get them. When they awoke it was dark. Hansel said to his sister, "Wait till the moon is up, then we shall see the bread I dropped on the ground. The bread will show us the way home."

The moon rose, but they could see no bread. The birds in the woods had eaten every piece. The children still tried to find the way home. They walked the whole night and all the next day, but they were still in the woods. They were tired and hungry, and they lay down under a tree and fell asleep.

■part 图地域　■walk along 歩く　■go by（時が）過ぎる　■show ~ a way ~に道を示す　■lie down 横になる

ヘンゼルとグレーテル

　おかみさんは子どもたちをどんどん森の奥まで連れていった。そこは、子どもたちがこれまで来たことのないところだった。前と同じように、大きなたき火が作られると、継母が言った。「ここにいるんだよ、おまえたち。くたびれたら寝てもいいよ。わたしたちはもっと奥へ行って、木を切って来るよ。それが終わったら、迎えに来るからね」

　お昼になると、グレーテルは自分のパンをヘンゼルとわけ合って食べた。ヘンゼルが歩きながらパンを地面にまいてしまったからだ。それから、2人は眠り込んだ。夕方になってもだれも迎えに来なかった。2人が目覚めると、まっ暗な夜になっていた。兄は妹に言った。「お月様が出るまで待つんだよ。そうすれば、地面にまいておいたパンくずが見えるからね。パンくずが家に帰る道を教えてくれるよ」

　月が昇ったが、パンくずを見つけることができなかった。森の鳥たちが全部食べてしまったのだ。それでも、子どもたちは家に帰る道を見つけようとした。夜通し歩き、次の日も1日じゅう歩いた。けれども森から出ることはできなかった。2人は疲れ切っておなかがすいたので、木の下で横になり、眠り込んだ。

Hansel and Gretel

The next day they walked more. They both knew that they were deep in the woods. If help did not come soon they would die. Then they saw a beautiful snow-white bird sitting on a branch. It was singing so beautifully that they stopped to listen. When it finished its song, the bird flew in front of them. They followed it until it landed on the roof of a little house. It was a strange-looking house. When the children got closer they were happy to see that the house was built of bread. Its roof was made of cake and its windows were made of sugar.

"Okay," Hansel said, "let's have a good meal for a change. I will have a piece of the roof, and you have a nice, sweet window."

Hansel picked off a piece of the roof and began eating. Gretel stood by a window and ate some of it. Then a voice called from inside:

"Who's eating my house?"

The children answered:

"The wind, the wind, the child of heaven," and quietly continued eating.

■snow-white 形雪のように白い　■land 動着地する　■get closer より近づく　■meal 名食事　■for a change 趣向を変えて　■pick off つかみ取る　■heaven 名天

ヘンゼルとグレーテル

　次の日、2人はさらに歩いた。自分たちが森の奥深くにいることに気づいていた。すぐに助けが来なければ、死んでしまうだろう。そのとき、雪のように白いきれいな鳥が、枝に止まっているのが見えた。あまりに美しく歌うので、2人は立ち止まって聞きほれた。その鳥は歌い終えると、2人の前を飛んでいった。そのあとについていくと、鳥は小さな家の屋根に止まった。それは奇妙な形をした家だった。近づいて家を見ると、子どもたちは喜んだ。その家はパンで作られていて、屋根はケーキで葺かれ、窓は砂糖でできていたのだ。

　「ようし」ヘンゼルが言った。「たまには、おいしいごはんを食べよう。ぼくは屋根を一かけら食べるから、おまえはおいしそうな甘い窓を食べてごらん」

　ヘンゼルは屋根を一かけらはずして、食べはじめた。グレーテルは窓の外に立ち、少し食べてみた。すると、家のなかから声がした。

　「わたしの家をかじるのは、だれだい？」

　子どもたちが答えた。

　「風だよ、風だよ。天の子だ」。そう答えると、だまって食べ続けた。

Hansel and Gretel

Hansel thought the roof tasted very good. He tore off another big piece. Gretel took out the window and sat down to eat it. Suddenly the door opened and an old woman came out. Hansel and Gretel shook with fright. They dropped their food.

The old woman said, "Dear children, who brought you here? Come in and stay with me. You are safe with me!"

She took them by the hand and led them into the house. Inside, a good dinner was ready; milk, cakes, fruit and many other things the children had never even seen before. Afterwards, two little white beds were uncovered. Hansel and Gretel lay down in them and felt like they were in heaven.

The old woman, however, was not nice. She was really a witch. She caught the children who came to her house. After she caught them, she killed them. Then she cooked and ate them. The witch could not see far, but she had a good sense of smell. She could smell humans from far away. As soon as Hansel and Gretel came near her house, she had laughed, and said to herself, "I'll have them—they shall not escape."

■tore 動tear（引きはがす）の過去　■fright 名恐怖　■dear 形かわいい　■uncover 動覆いを取る　■afterwards 副その後　■witch 名魔女　■as soon as ～する途端

ヘンゼルとグレーテル

　ヘンゼルは、屋根はとてもおいしいと思い、また大きな一かけらを引きはがした。グレーテルは窓を取りはずし、座り込んで食べた。すると、いきなり戸が開いて、おばあさんが出てきた。2人はぎょっとして、食べ物を落としてしまった。

　おばあさんが言った。「子どもたちや、だれに連れられて来たのかね？　なかにお入り。わたしといれば、心配することなんかありゃしないよ」
　おばあさんは子どもたちの手を取り、家に入った。家のなかにはすばらしいごちそうが用意されていた——ミルク、ケーキ、果物、それに子どもたちが見たこともないたくさんの食べ物もあった。ごちそうを食べてしまうと、2つの小さなベッドの白いシーツがめくられた。ヘンゼルとグレーテルはベッドに横になり、天国にいるような気分がした。

　ところが、おばあさんは親切そうなふりをしているだけで、実は魔女だった。自分の家にやって来る子どもたちをつかまえ、そのあとで殺してしまう。それから煮て食べてしまうのだ。魔女は遠くをよく見ることができなかったが、鼻はよく利き、遠くからでも人間のにおいがわかった。ヘンゼルとグレーテルが家に近寄って来た途端、魔女は笑って、ひとりごとを言った。「あいつらをつかまえよう——逃してなるものか」

Hansel and Gretel

🎧03 Early the next morning, before the children were awake, the witch got up. When she saw their round, red faces, she thought, "What a tasty dish!" Then she grabbed Hansel and carried him to a little stable. She put him inside it and he could not escape. He shouted as loudly as he could, but it was no use. Next, the witch went to Gretel and cried, "Get up girl, and get some water to cook your brother something nice; he is outside in the stable and must be fattened up. When he is fat enough I shall eat him."

Gretel began to cry, but she was forced to do what the old witch told her to do.

From then on, Hansel was given lots of good food, but Gretel got only dry bread. Every morning the old witch went to the stable and said, "Hansel, put your finger out so that I can feel how fat you are getting." Hansel would put out a bone instead of a finger. The old woman, because she could not see well, wondered why Hansel did not grow fat.

After four weeks, Hansel was still thin. The witch decided she would wait no longer.

■dish 名料理 ■grab 動ひっつかむ ■stable 名家畜小屋 ■no use まったく役に立たない ■fatten up 太らせる ■force to do 強制的にやらせる ■from then on それ以来 ■thin 形やせた

ヘンゼルとグレーテル

　次の朝早く、子どもたちが目覚める前に、魔女は起きた。子どもたちのふっくらとした赤い顔を見て、「何てうまそうなごちそうだろう！」と思った。そしてヘンゼルをひっつかむと、小さな家畜小屋まで運んだ。そこにヘンゼルを入れて、逃げられないようにした。ヘンゼルはあらん限りの大声で叫んだが、何の役にも立たなかった。次に、魔女はグレーテルのところに行き、怒鳴った。「起きるんだよ。おまえの兄さんにごちそうを作るための水をくんで来るんだ。兄さんは外の家畜小屋に入れてある。太らせる必要があるんだよ。十分に太ったら、わたしが食べるのさ」

　グレーテルは泣き出したが、年取った魔女に言いつけられたことをするよりほかはなかった。

　それ以来、ヘンゼルはごちそうをたくさん与えられたが、グレーテルは乾いたパンしかもらえなかった。毎朝、年取った魔女は家畜小屋に行き、言った。「ヘンゼル、指をお出し。おまえがどれだけ太ったかわかるからにね」。ヘンゼルは指を出す代わりに骨を差し出した。年取った魔女は目が悪いので、どうしてヘンゼルは太らないのだろうと、いぶかしく思った。

　4週間たっても、ヘンゼルはやせたままだった。魔女はこれ以上待つ気がなくなった。

Hansel and Gretel

"Whether Hansel is fat or thin, I will kill and eat him tomorrow!"

The tears ran down the face of poor little Gretel.

"Dear God, help us!" she prayed. "If the wild animals had eaten us in the woods we would at least have died together."

When the witch had gone, Gretel ran to Hansel and told him what the witch had said.

"We must escape somehow. If we don't she will kill us both."

Hansel said, "I know how to get out. I have loosened the window. But first you must get her magic wand so we can save ourselves if she follows us. Bring the flute that hangs in her room as well."

Gretel got both the wand and the flute, and the children escaped.

When the old witch came to see whether her dinner was ready, she saw they had escaped. She ran angrily to the window. Though her eyes were bad, she could see the children running away.

■run down 流れ落ちる　■pray 動祈る　■somehow 副どうにかして　■loosen 動ゆるめる　■wand 名杖　■as well おまけに、その上　■though 接 ～にもかかわらず

ヘンゼルとグレーテル

「ヘンゼルが太っていようがやせていようが、明日はあいつを殺して食べてやろう！」

かわいそうな小さなグレーテルの目から涙が流れた。

「神様、お助けください！」グレーテルは祈った。「森のなかで、けものに食べられたのなら、少なくとも兄さんといっしょに死ねたのに」

魔女が行ってしまうと、グレーテルはヘンゼルのところに走っていき、魔女の言ったことを知らせた。

「何とか逃げなくちゃならないわ。そうしなければ、2人とも殺されてしまう」

ヘンゼルが答えた。「逃げ方はわかっているよ。窓をゆるめておいたんだ。でも、最初に、魔法の杖を手に入れるんだ。魔女につけられたときに自分たちを守るためにね。それと、部屋にかかっている笛も持ち出すんだよ」

グレーテルが杖と笛を手に入れると、2人は逃げ出した。

年取った魔女が食事の準備ができているか見に来ると、子どもたちが逃げたことに気がついた。怒って窓に走りよると、目は悪いけれど、子どもたちが逃げていくのが見えた。

Hansel and Gretel

She quickly put on her magic shoes. The shoes could cover several yards with each step. She quickly caught up with the children. Gretel, however, had seen her coming. She used the magic wand and turned Hansel into a lake. She turned herself into a swan and stayed in the middle of the lake. The witch sat on the shore and tried to get the swan to come to her by throwing pieces of bread to it. Gretel did not go near, and at last the witch went home without the children.

Then Gretel used the wand to change herself and Hansel back, and they traveled on through the night. Gretel then turned herself into a beautiful rose in the middle of a thorny hedge, and Hansel sat by the side.

Soon the witch came along. She acted as if she did not know Hansel.

"Young man," she said, "may I pick that beautiful rose?"

"Oh yes," said Hansel.

■cover 動（ある範囲に）及ぶ　■yard 名ヤード《91.44cm》　■turn ~ into ~を…に変える　■shore 名沿岸　■thorny 形イバラの　■hedge 名生垣　■as if あたかも~のように

ヘンゼルとグレーテル

　魔女は急いで魔法の靴をはいた。その靴をはくと1歩ごとに数ヤード進むことができ、すぐに子どもたちに追いついた。ところが、グレーテルには魔女がやって来るのが見えたので、魔法の杖でヘンゼルを湖に変えた。自分は白鳥に姿を変え、湖のまんなかに浮かんだ。魔女は岸辺に座り、白鳥にパンくずを投げて自分のほうに近づかせようとした。グレーテルはそばに行かなかったので、魔女は子どもたちをつかまえることができず、とうとうひとりで家に帰っていった。

　グレーテルは杖を使って自分たちを元の姿に戻し、2人は夜通し森のなかを歩いた。そのあとグレーテルは、イバラのやぶのまんなかにある美しいバラに姿を変え、ヘンゼルはやぶの脇に座った。

　すぐに、魔女がやって来たが、ヘンゼルのことをまったく知らないように振る舞った。
　「そこの若い方」魔女が言った。「あの美しいバラをつんでもいいかい？」
　「もちろんですとも」ヘンゼルが答えた。

Hansel and Gretel

She went to the hedge in a hurry to gather the flower, knowing that it was Gretel. Hansel pulled out his flute and began to play. The flute was a magic flute. Whoever heard the flute had to dance whether he wanted to dance or not. The old witch was forced to dance on and on. She could not stop to pick the rose. The thorns tore the clothes from her body and caught in her skin. Finally, she could not move.

Then Gretel used the magic wand to set herself free again and she and Hansel set out for home. After traveling a long way, Gretel grew tired. Both the children lay down to sleep. As they slept, the witch, who had escaped from the thorny hedge, came by. Seeing her magic wand, she picked it up and turned poor Hansel into a deer. She then decided to leave them in the woods to be eaten by wild animals. It was too much trouble to try and get them to her house again.

When Gretel woke and found what had happened she cried for poor Hansel. Beside her, tears rolled from Hansel's eyes, too.

Gretel said, "Rest, little deer; I will never leave you."

■in a hurry 急いで ■whether ~ or not ~にしろそうでないにしろ ■on and on 延々と ■set ~ free ~を自由の身にする ■come by やって来る ■deer 名シカ ■poor 形かわいそうな ■roll 動流れる

ヘンゼルとグレーテル

　魔女は急いでやぶのほうに行き、花を取ろうとした。それがグレーテルだとわかっていたからだ。ヘンゼルは笛を引っ張り出し、吹きはじめた。それは魔法の笛だったので、その音を聞くとだれでも望もうと望むまいと、踊り出すようになっていた。年取った魔女も延々と踊るしかなかった。そのため、立ち止まって花をつむことができなかった。イバラのとげが魔女の服を引き裂き、肌を刺したので、とうとう、魔女は動けなくなった。

　すると、グレーテルは魔法の杖でふたたび元の姿に戻り、ヘンゼルと家に向けて出発した。長い道のりを進んだあと、グレーテルはすっかりくたびれてしまった。２人は横になって寝ることにした。眠っていると、イバラのやぶから逃れた魔女がやって来た。魔法の杖を見つけると、それを持ち上げ、かわいそうなことにヘンゼルをシカに変えてしまった。そこで魔女は、子どもたちを森にほうって置き、けものたちの餌食にすることにした。もう一度２人を自分の家に連れ帰るのは、こりごりだったのだ。

　グレーテルは目を覚まして何が起こったか気づくと、かわいそうなヘンゼルのために泣き出した。その横にいるヘンゼルの目からも、涙が流れ落ちた。
　グレーテルは言った。「シカさん、安心して。決してあなたを見捨てないからね」

Hansel and Gretel

She took the poor deer with her as she tried to find her way home. At last they came to a little house. When Gretel found that no one lived there she decided she and Hansel would stay there.

She made a soft bed for the deer. Each morning she went out and gathered food for both of them. The deer ate out of her hand, and they played happily together. In the evening, when Gretel was tired, she laid her head on the deer and slept. If Hansel had had his own body they would have led a very happy life.

They lived like this for years and Gretel became a young woman. One day the king came to hunt there. When the deer heard the noise of the hunt, the dogs, the horses and the huntsmen, he wanted to see what was going on.

"Oh sister," he said, "let me go into the woods, so I can see what is happening."

He asked so often that at last Gretel let him go.

"But," she said, "be sure to come back in the evening. I shall close the door to keep out the huntsmen, but if you tap and say, 'Sister, let me in,' I shall know it is you. If you do not speak, I shall keep the door closed."

■each morning 毎朝　■eat out of hand 手で直接食べる　■hunt 動 狩りをする　■be sure to 必ず〜してください　■keep out 入らせない　■tap 動 軽くたたく

ヘンゼルとグレーテル

　グレーテルはかわいそうなシカを連れて、家に帰る道を見つけようとした。とうとう2人は、ある小さな家のところまで来た。グレーテルはそこにだれも住んでいないことを見て取ると、ヘンゼルとそこに留まることにした。

　グレーテルはシカのために柔らかな寝床を作ってやった。毎朝、外に出かけ、2人の食べ物を集めた。シカは妹の手から食べさせてもらい、いっしょに楽しく遊んだ。日が暮れてグレーテルがくたびれると、頭をシカにのせて眠った。ヘンゼルが人間の姿さえしていたなら、2人はとても幸せに暮らせたことだろう。

　こんなふうにして2人は長年過ごし、グレーテルは若い娘になった。ある日、王様が森に狩りにやって来た。狩りの物音や、犬や馬の鳴き声、それに猟師たちのかけ声を聞くと、シカは何が起こっているのか見たくなった。

　「ねえ、妹よ」シカが言った。「森の奥に行かせてくれないか。どうなっているか見たいんだ」

　シカがしつこく頼むので、とうとうグレーテルは行かせてやることにした。

　「でもね」妹が言った。「日暮れにはきっと戻って来てね。猟師が入ってこないように、戸に鍵をかけておくわ。でも、帰ってきたら兄さんだとわかるように、戸をたたいて『妹よ、入れておくれ』と言ってね。そう言わなければ、戸をあけないわ」

Hansel and Gretel

Hansel ran away as fast as he could, jumping high in the air in his happiness. The king and his huntsmen followed the beautiful animal, but could not catch him. Each time they thought they had him he would jump over a hedge and be out of sight again.

When it was dark Hansel ran home and said, "Sister, let me in!" Gretel opened the door and he jumped in. He was soon sleeping soundly on his soft bed.

Next morning the hunt continued and when he heard the noise, the deer said, "Sister, open the door. I must go."

Once again the king and huntsmen followed the little deer. The hunt lasted all day. Near evening one of the hunters hit the deer in the foot. Although he was hurt, Hansel got home before he was caught. The hunter followed Hansel and heard the little deer say, "Sister, let me in." The man saw the deer go inside the house. The huntsman ran to the king and told him what he had seen.

"Tomorrow," said the king, "we shall have another hunt and this time we shall catch this deer."

Gretel was very upset when she saw that Hansel was hurt. She washed the blood away and put some magic on his foot. Then they went to sleep.

■out of sight 見えないところに　■soundly 副 ぐっすりと　■last 動 続く　■hurt 形 けがをした　■upset 形 取り乱して

ヘンゼルとグレーテル

　ヘンゼルは思いっきり速く走り、うれしくなって高く跳び上がった。王様と猟師たちは、この美しいけものを追いかけたが、つかまえることはできなかった。とらえたと思うごとに、シカはやぶを跳び越えて、ふたたび見えなくなってしまった。

　暗くなると、ヘンゼルは家に帰り、「妹よ、入れておくれ」と言った。グレーテルが戸をあけると、なかに跳び込んだ。そしてすぐに、やわらかな寝床でぐっすりと眠った。

　次の朝も狩りは続き、その物音を聞くとシカが言った。「妹よ、戸をあけてくれないか。行かずにはいられないよ」

　またもや、王様と猟師たちは小さなシカを追った。狩りは1日じゅう続いた。日が暮れるころ、ひとりの猟師がシカの足に傷を負わせた。ヘンゼルは怪我をしたが、つかまらずに家に着いた。あとをつけた猟師は、小さなシカが「妹よ、入れておくれ」と言うのを聞き、家に入るのを見届けた。猟師は王様の元に駆けつけ、自分の見たことを話した。

　「明日も」王様が言った。「もう一度狩りをして、今度こそ、きっとシカをつかまえてみせる」

　グレーテルはヘンゼルの怪我を見て、とても驚いた。血を洗い流し、足に少し魔法をかけた。そして、2人は眠った。

Hansel and Gretel

In the morning there was no mark anywhere on the deer's foot. When Hansel heard the hunt starting again he said, "I must go Gretel, but I will take care they don't catch me."

But Gretel was still upset from the night before.

"I am sure they will kill you this time: I will not let you go."

"I shall die," said Hansel, "if you keep me here." Gretel was not happy but she had to let him go, and he quickly ran off into the woods.

When the king saw the deer he said to his men, "Follow him all day long until you catch him, but do not hurt him." The deer was too fast for them, however. When evening came, the king told his men to stop.

"Show me where the little house is," he said to the man who had followed the deer the day before. When they got to the house the king knocked on the door and said "Sister, let me in."

The door opened and the king went in. He saw the most beautiful girl he had ever seen.

■mark 图（傷などの）跡　■take care 気をつける　■night before 昨夜　■run off 走り去る

ヘンゼルとグレーテル

　朝になると、シカの傷跡はすっかり消えていた。ヘンゼルは狩りがふたたびはじまる物音を聞くと、言った。「行かなきゃならない、グレーテル。でも、つかまらないように注意するよ」

　ところが、グレーテルは昨夜からずっと不安でたまらなかった。
「今度はきっと殺されてしまうわ。行かせてあげるわけにいかない」

「ぼくは死んでしまうよ」ヘンゼルが言い返した。「行かせてくれないならね」。グレーテルが重い心でシカを外に出してやると、シカは急いで森の奥に駆けていった。
　王様はシカを見つけると、猟師たちに言った。「１日じゅうシカをつけて、つかまえろ。だが、傷つけてはいけない」。ところが、猟師たちにはシカの足はあまりに速すぎた。日が沈むと、王様は狩りをやめるように命じた。
「小さな家がどこにあるか案内してくれ」王様は、前日にシカのあとをつけた猟師に言った。その家に着くと、王様は戸をたたいて、「妹よ、入れておくれ」と言った。

　戸があき、王様はなかに入った。そこにはこれまで見たことのない美しい娘がいた。

Hansel and Gretel

Gretel was very frightened when she saw that it was not the deer but a king who had entered her house, but the king spoke kindly. After a while he took her hand and said, "Will you come to my palace and be my wife?"

"Yes," replied Gretel, "I will come to your palace but I cannot be your wife, and my deer must go with me for I cannot part with him."

"Well," said the king, "he shall come and live with you all your life. He will have everything he wants."

Just then the little deer came home. Soon, everyone was ready to leave. The king lifted Gretel onto his horse and they rode to his palace. The deer ran happily behind them. On the way Gretel told the king her story. He knew the old witch and her bad ways and sent for her the next day. He ordered her to change the deer back into human form.

When she saw her dear brother again Gretel was very thankful. She agreed to marry the king. They lived happily for the rest of their lives. Hansel became the king's right-hand man.

■frightened 形 怯えた　■palace 名 宮殿　■part with 〜と別れる　■bad way きたないやり口　■send for（人）を呼びに行かせる　■right-hand man 腹心、右腕となる人

ヘンゼルとグレーテル

　グレーテルは、家に入って来たのがシカではなく王様だったので、ひどく怯えたが、王様はやさしく話しかけた。しばらくすると、王様は娘の手を取って言った。「わたしの城に来て、妻になってくれないか？」

　「はい」グレーテルは答えた。「あなたの城に参りますが、妻にはなれません。それにシカもいっしょでないと困ります。離れるわけにはいかないのです」

　「なるほど」王様が言った。「シカも連れて来て、いつまでもあなたのそばに置いてもかまわない。シカにはほしいものは何でもさずけよう」

　ちょうどそのとき、小さなシカが戻って来た。まもなく、みんなの出発の用意が整った。王様はグレーテルを自分の馬に乗せ、城まで連れていった。シカはそのあとをうれしそうに追いかけた。途中で、グレーテルは王様にこれまでのことを話した。王様は年を取った魔女と、その邪悪なやり口を知っていて、次の日、魔女を呼びにやらせた。そして王様は魔女にシカを人間の姿に戻すように命じた。

　グレーテルは、愛する兄の姿をふたたび見て、感謝の気持ちで一杯になり、王様の求婚に応じた。王様とお后は残りの人生を幸せに送り、ヘンゼルは王様の腹心の部下になった。

覚えておきたい英語表現

> they *stopped to* listen. (p. 26, 5行目)
> 彼らは聴くために立ち止まった。

stop to V は「V するために立ち止まる」という意味です（V は verb の略）。似た表現に stop Ving「V するのをやめる」があります。

　　　　He *stopped smoking*.　　　　彼はタバコを吸うのをやめた（中断した）。
　　　　He *stopped to* smoke.　　　　彼はタバコを吸うために立ち止まった。

意味が正反対ですね。しっかり区別しておかなければ間違えてしまいますから注意してください。ちなみに stop は「進行中の動作を中断する」という意味の「やめる」です。禁煙という意味であれば "quit smoking" を使います。

さて、似た用法に以下のようなものがあります。

　　　　I *remember mailing* the letter.　　　手紙を投函した覚えがある。
　　　　Please *remember to* mail the letter!　　忘れずに手紙を投函してね！

覚え方がややこしいですね。私は生徒に「to は未来志向のイメージ」と説明します。不定詞として多用される to ですが、英会話では用法を考えていては間に合わないこともあります。そんな時のためにも「to は未来志向！」でぜひ理解してみてください。

　　　He stopped　　　/　　→ to　　　smoke.
　　　彼は止まった　　　/　　→ その後　　タバコを吸った

　　　Please remember　/　　→ to　　　mail the letter.
　　　覚えておいて　　　/　　→ この後で　手紙を投函する

一方、現在分詞（Ving）は過去志向です。"He is playing the piano." は「彼はピアノを弾いているところだ」という意味ですから、すでに play（弾く）という動作は「目の前で行われた」のです。「Ving は過去志向」と覚えるとよいでしょう。

ちなみにPart2のThe Frog Princeに"〜 ***stop*** your ***crying*** right now,"(p. 52)という表現が出てきます。cry「泣く」という行為はすでに行われていて、それをやめてほしい、という意味になるのがお分かりいただけるでしょう。

しつこいですが「toは未来志向」「Vingは過去志向」が合言葉です！

> "Sister, *let me in.*" (p. 38, 20行目)
> 妹よ、中に入れておくれ。

let + 人or物 + 前置詞（副詞）で「〜を…の状態にさせる」という意味です。let + 人or物 + 動詞で「〜に…させる」という意味で用いる、「使役動詞」としてのletが文法学習ではポピュラーですが、どちらも慣れておくと大変便利です。簡単な表現ですが、日常会話でよく使う表現です。ぜひ覚えましょう。

【例文】

Let me know.	私にも教えて。
Let me out!	出してくれ！（Part 2 The Bottled Spirit p. 68参照）
Let me go with you.	君と一緒に行きたいな。
Let me try.	私にもやらせて。
Let me alone.	一人にさせて。
Let me have a look.	ちょっと見せて。
Let me pay.	私に支払わせて。

「Let me 〜」は「私に〜させてください」という直訳なので、日本語で考えると少々固い表現にも思えます。状況にもよりますが、ネイティブの使い方としては「ちょっと〜していい？」「〜させてね」くらいのニュアンスです。あまり堅苦しく考えずに気楽に使ってみましょう。丁寧に言いたい時にはPleaseを付け加えればOKです。

Part 2

The Frog Prince
カエルの王子

The Bottled Spirit
瓶のなかのお化け

The Three Spinning Women
糸を紡ぐ三人の女

The Frog Prince

In the good old days, when wishes often came true, there lived a king. All his daughters were beautiful. The youngest princess was so beautiful that even the sun was surprised every time it kissed her face.

Close to the king's home was a dark forest. In the forest under an old tree was a waterhole. The princess often went to the waterhole on hot days. She sat on the bank by the cool water. She loved playing with a special golden ball. She would throw the ball high in the air and then catch it.

■come true（願いなどが）かなう　■close to ～の近くに　■waterhole 名泉
■bank 名岸　■would 助 ～したものだった

カエルの王子

　古きよき時代、しばしば人の願いごとがかなったころ、王様がいた。王様には娘がいて、いずれも美しかった。とりわけ末の娘は美しく、太陽でさえ、その顔を照らすたびに驚いたくらいだった。

　王様の城の近くに、暗い森があった。森のなかの古い木の下に泉が湧いていた。末の姫は、暑い日にはたびたび泉のところまで行った。そして、冷たい泉のほとりに腰かけた。姫はお気に入りの金のまりで遊ぶのが好きで、まりを空高く投げ上げては、また受け止めて遊んでいた。

The Frog Prince

One day, instead of falling into her little hands, the princess' golden ball rolled along the ground into the water. The princess went to the well to look for her ball. The well was so deep, however, that she could not see the bottom. She began to cry. She cried louder and louder. Then a voice called out, "Why, princess, what is the matter? You cry so loudly even a stone would feel sorry for you." She looked round to see who was talking and saw a frog with its head sticking out of the water.

The frog was not very pretty, but the princess told him about her problem.

"Well, stop your crying right now," said the frog, "I can help you. What will you give me if I get your ball for you?"

"Anything you like, my dear frog," she said: "I would give you my clothes, my riches, or even my crown."

■instead of 〜の代わりに　■well 名泉　■stick out 突き出す　■rich 形《-es》富
■crown 名王冠

カエルの王子

　ある日のこと、金のまりは姫の小さな手のなかに落ちて来ずに、地面を転がって水のなかに落ちてしまった。姫は泉まで行って、まりを捜した。ところが泉はとても深く、底が見えなかった。姫は泣き出し、泣き声はどんどん大きくなった。すると、呼びかける声がした。「おや、お姫様、どうしたの？　そんなに大声で泣かれると、石でさえあなたを気の毒に思いますよ」。姫はあたりを見回して、だれがしゃべっているのか見つけようとした。すると、カエルが頭を水から突き出しているのが見えた。

　カエルはあまりきれいな姿とは言えなかったが、姫は、まりが落ちて困っていると話した。
　「それでは、今すぐ泣くのをおやめなさい」カエルが言った。「わたしが助けてあげましょう。まりを取って来てあげたら、わたしに何をくださいますか？」
　「何でも望みの物をあげるわ、カエルさん」姫は答えた。「わたしの服、宝物、それに王冠だってあげる」

The Frog Prince

The frog thought about this for a moment and then said, "Thank you princess, but I don't want any of these things. What I want is your love. I want to be your friend. I want you to play with me and to let me sit next to you at your table. Let me eat off your plate and share your little bed with you. If you do, I will get your golden ball from the bottom of the well."

"Okay," she said. "I'll promise anything you like if you get my ball back for me." The frog disappeared into the well and the princess thought, "What a fool the frog is! He can only sit in the water and talk to other frogs, he can't be friends with humans."

In a little while the frog came back with the ball in his mouth. He threw it to the princess. She was so happy to get it back. She picked it up and ran away.

"Stop! Stop! Take me with you, I can't run so fast," shouted the little frog. It was no use. Even though he shouted as loudly as he could the princess ignored him. Soon she got home and she quickly forgot all about the little frog who had helped her. The frog sadly went back into his well.

■want someone to 人に〜してほしい　■eat off a plate 皿から取って食べる　■what a fool なんて愚かな　■pick up 拾い上げる　■ignore 動 〜に気づかないふりをする

カエルの王子

　カエルは姫の答えをしばらく考えて、言った。「ありがとう、お姫様。でも、そんなものは何もほしくありません。あなたの愛がほしいのです。お友だちになってほしいのです。わたしと遊んで、食卓では隣に座らせてほしいのです。あなたのお皿から料理を食べさせてもらい、あなたの小さなベッドでいっしょに寝たいのです。そうしてくださるのなら、泉の底から金のまりを取って来て差し上げます」

　「いいわ」姫は答えた。「まりを取って来てくれたら、何でも望みをかなえてあげると約束するわ」。カエルが水のなかに姿を消すと、姫は考えた。「なんて愚かなカエルでしょう！　水につかって、ほかのカエルたちとしゃべっていればいいんだわ。人間と友だちになんかなれるわけがない」

　しばらくすると、カエルが口にまりをくわえて戻って来た。それを姫のほうに投げた。姫は、まりが戻ってひどく喜び、拾い上げると駆け出した。
　「お待ちください！　お待ちください！　わたしを連れていってくださいな。そんなに速く走れませんよ」小さなカエルが叫んだが、何の役にも立たなかった。どんなに大声で叫んでも、姫は聞こえないふりをした。まもなく家に着くと、すぐに自分を助けてくれた小さなカエルのことなどすっかり忘れてしまった。カエルは悲しそうに泉に戻っていった。

The Frog Prince

The next day the princess sat down to eat with the king and the rest of her family. She was eating off her little gold dish when she heard a strange noise. Something jumped up the stairs, knocked on the door and said, "Young princess, let me in!" She ran to the door and saw the frog. She shut the door quickly and went back to her seat. She was very afraid.

The king saw this and said, "Child, why are you afraid? What is at the door?"

"A frog," she answered.

"What does the frog want with you?" asked the king.

"Well, dear father, yesterday, when I was playing in the forest, my golden ball fell into the well. I started crying and the frog heard me. He got the ball back for me. I promised him he could be my friend, but I never thought he would come so far out of his water. Now he is outside and wants to come in." There was another knock at the door and the frog called:

■rest of 他の ■let me in 私を中に入れてください ■get ~ back ~を取り戻す
■never thought ~なんて思ってもみなかった

カエルの王子

　次の日、姫は食卓に着いて、王様や家族と食事をしていた。小さな金のお皿から食べていると、奇妙な音が聞こえてきた。ぺしゃり、ぺたりと、何かが跳んで階段を上がって来て、戸をたたいて、言った。「末のお姫様。わたしを入れてください！」。姫が戸まで走っていくと、カエルが見えた。姫はすぐに戸を閉めて自分の席に戻ったが、とても怯えていた。

　これを見た王様がたずねた。「おまえ、どうしてそんなに怯えているのだ？　戸のところに何がいるんだい？」
「カエルです」姫が答えた。
「カエルはおまえに何を望んでいるのだね？」王様がたずねた。
「あのね、お父様、きのう森で遊んでいると、金のまりが泉に落ちたの。泣いていると、カエルがわたしの泣き声に気づいて、まりを取り戻してくれました。それで、カエルに友だちになってあげると約束しました。でも、カエルが水から上がって出て来ることができるなんて思ってもみなかったわ。今、カエルが部屋の外にいて、入りたがっているのです」。またもや戸をたたく音がして、カエルが叫んだ。

The Frog Prince

"Open the door, my princess, dear,
Open the door to your true love here!
Remember the promise you yesterday made
By the cool well, in the old tree's shade."

Then the king said, "You must not break your promise. Go and let him in."

She went and opened the door, and the frog jumped in. He followed her to her chair and said, "Lift me up."

She did not want to lift him up, but the king ordered her to do so. The frog got onto the table and said, "Push your little gold dish near me so that we can eat together." The princess pushed her plate near the frog but she was not happy. The frog ate a lot, but the princess ate nothing. At last the frog said, "I am full. Now I am tired. Take me to your little room, put me in your bed and we will lie down and go to sleep."

The princess began to cry. She could not bring herself even to touch the cold frog. She did not want him sleeping in her pretty, clean bed.

■shade 图木陰　■lift ~ up ~を持ち上げる　■order 動命令する　■full 形満腹の
■bring oneself to ~する気になる

カエルの王子

「戸をあけてください、いとしいお姫様
　あなたの真実の愛に通じる戸をあけてください
　きのうの約束をお忘れですか
　木陰の冷たい泉のそばの約束を」

　すると、王様が言った。「約束を破ってはいけない。行って、戸をあけてあげなさい」
　姫が行って、戸をあけると、カエルがぴょんぴょんと入って来た。カエルは姫のあとについて椅子まで来て、言った。「食卓にのせてください」
　姫はカエルをのせたくなかったが、王様はそうするように命じた。カエルは食卓にのると言った。「あなたの小さな金のお皿をわたしのほうに寄せてください。そうすればいっしょに食べられますから」。姫は皿をカエルのほうに押したが、いやでたまらなかった。カエルはたくさん食べたが、姫は一口も食べなかった。最後にカエルが言った。「おなかが一杯です。そろそろ疲れてきました。わたしをあなたの小さな部屋に連れていって、ベッドに寝かせてくださいな。そしていっしょに横になって眠りましょう」
　姫は泣き出した。冷たいカエルをさわる気にもなれなかったのだ。それに、きれいで清潔な自分のベッドにカエルを寝かせたくなかった。

The Frog Prince

The king became angry with her and said, "We must not forget the people who have helped us."

So, the princess lifted up the frog, carried him upstairs and put him in a corner of her room. When she was in bed the frog came over to her and said, "I am tired, I would like to go to bed too. Lift me up, please, or I'll tell your father." Then the princess got really angry. She picked the frog up and threw him against the wall.

"You bad frog," she shouted.

When he fell to the ground, however, he was no longer a frog. He was a prince, with beautiful, smiling eyes. He told the princess how an old witch had changed him into a frog. Nobody except the young princess had the power to change him back.

■upstairs 副上の階へ ■come over to ～にやって来る ■nobody except ～の他は誰も（ない） ■change ～ back ～を元に戻す

カエルの王子

　王様は姫の態度に怒って言った。「助けてくれた人をないがしろにしてはいけないぞ」

　そういうわけで、姫はカエルを持ち上げ、上の階に連れていき、自分の部屋の隅に置いた。姫がベッドに入ると、カエルがはい寄って来て語りかけた。「疲れました。わたしもベッドで横になりたいです。どうかわたしを持ち上げてください。さもないと、父上に言いつけますよ」。それを聞いて姫はしんから腹を立てた。カエルをつかみ上げると、壁に投げつけた。

　「ろくでもないカエルめ」姫が叫んだ。

　ところが、床に落ちたカエルはもはやカエルの姿をしていなかった。きれいな、にこやかな目をした王子になっていた。王子は姫に、自分は年を取った魔女にカエルに変えられ、元の姿に戻せるのは末の姫様のほかにいなかったのだと話して聞かせた。

The Frog Prince

"Tomorrow we will travel back to my kingdom together," he said. They slept happily, and when the sun came up the next morning, a carriage with eight white horses arrived at the door. Behind the horses stood Henry, the faithful servant of the young prince. Henry was so upset when his master was turned into a frog. Henry had put three rings of iron around his heart to stop it breaking from sadness.

The carriage set off for the prince's land with the prince and the princess happy together inside the carriage and Henry outside, driving. They had not gone far when the young couple heard a noise as if something was breaking. They heard the same noise three times. They thought something in the carriage had broken. However, when they looked outside they saw that it was only the iron rings breaking from Henry's heart, because he was so happy.

■carriage 名大型の馬車　■faithful 形忠実な　■servant 名家来　■set off 出発する

カエルの王子

　「明日、いっしょにわたしの国に戻りましょう」と王子が言い、2人は幸せに眠った。次の朝、日が昇ると、八頭の白い馬に引かれた馬車が戸口に着いた。馬のうしろには、若い王子の忠義な家来、ヘンリーが立っていた。ヘンリーは主人がカエルに変えられてひどく心配し、胸のまわりに3本の鉄の輪をはめ、悲しみで胸が張り裂けないようにしていた。

　馬車は王子の国を目指して旅立った。馬車のなかでは王子と姫が幸せに座り、外ではヘンリーが馬車を走らせた。それほど遠くまで進まないうちに、若い2人は、何かが壊れるような音を聞いた。その音は3回続いた。2人は馬車のなかで何かが壊れたと思った。ところが外を見ると、その音は鉄の輪がヘンリーの胸からはじけた音だということがわかった。それほどまでにヘンリーはうれしかったのだ。

The Bottled Spirit

There was once a poor woodcutter who worked every day from early in the morning till late at night. After a long time he had saved a little money and he said to his son, "You are my only child, so I will give you the money I have made from my hard work. Spend it on your schooling. Learn something useful so you will be able to look after me when I am old."

The boy went to school and studied very hard. His teachers praised him for his work. After a few years he was able to go to college. Before he could complete his studies, however, he ran out of money and was forced to leave school. He returned to his father, who was very unhappy.

■spirit 名お化け ■there was once 昔々 ■schooling 名学校教育 ■praise 動 〜をほめる ■run out of 〜を使い果たす

瓶のなかのお化け

　むかしむかし、貧しい木こりがいた。木こりは毎日、朝早くから夜遅くまで働いた。長いあいだに、お金を少し貯めると、息子に言った。「おまえは、わしのたったひとりの子どもだ。おまえに、わしが汗水たらして稼いだお金をやろう。それを教育に使いなさい。役に立つことを学んで、わしが年を取ったときに面倒をみられるようにしておくれ」

　息子は学校に行き、一生懸命に勉強した。それで、先生たちに優秀な生徒だとほめられた。数年後には、大学に通えるようになった。ところが、学業を終える前にお金がなくなり、大学を去らなければならなくなった。学生が父親の元に戻ると、父親はとてもがっかりした。

The Bottled Spirit

"I have no more money," said the old woodcutter, "and the pay I get for woodcutting is only enough to buy food to eat."

"Don't worry father," answered the son, "If this is what God wants, it must be good."

The next day, the old man was getting ready to go to work. His son offered to go with him.

"Yes, my son, come; but it will be difficult for you. You are not used to such hard work. Also, I only have one ax."

"Never mind," said the son, "we will borrow an ax from our neighbor until I can buy a new one."

The neighbor kindly agreed and they set off together for the forest. All morning they worked and the son was pleased to be helping his father. The father was glad to have his son with him.

When the sun was at its highest the old man said, "We will rest now and have our lunch."

The son ate his bread but then instead of resting like his father, he walked in the forest. Everything was new and interesting to him.

■pay 名稼ぎ ■get ready to ～をする支度をする ■be not used to ～に慣れていない
■ax 名斧 ■never mind 心配しないで ■be glad to ～してうれしい

瓶のなかのお化け

「もうお金がないんだ」年老いた木こりが言った。「それに木こりをして稼いだお金では、食べ物を買うだけで精一杯だ」

「心配しないで、お父さん」息子が答えた。「これが神様の思し召しなら、きっといいことにちがいない」

次の日、年老いた木こりが仕事に行く支度をしていると、息子がいっしょに行きたいと言った。

「来てもかまわんがね、息子よ。だが、おまえには難しいだろう。こんなきつい仕事に慣れていないからな。それに、斧が一丁しかない」

「気にすることはないよ」息子が言った。「斧はお隣から借りてくる。新しいのを買ったら、返すことにするよ」

隣人は、親切にも斧を貸してくれ、親子は連れ立って森に出かけた。午前中ずっと２人は働き、息子は父親の手伝いができて喜んだ。父親は息子がいっしょに来てくれたことをうれしく思った。

日が一番高く昇ると、年老いた木こりが言った。「さあ、ここらで休んで昼飯を食べよう」

息子はパンを食べたが、そのあと父親のように休まず、森のなかに歩いていった。息子には、あらゆるものが新鮮で、面白かった。

The Bottled Spirit

"Where are you going, my son? You should rest and not tire yourself out."

"I won't go far, father. It's just that it feels good to be in the forest among the birds and trees."

He walked some more and came to a big old tree. He walked around the tree to get an idea of its size.

"Well, old tree, many birds have made their homes in your branches," he said quietly, as he looked up at the tree.

Then he thought he heard a voice. He listened very hard. He could just hear a voice saying, "Let me out! Let me out!"

He looked around but could see nothing so he called out. "Where are you? I can't see you."

"I'm over here," the voice answered, "in the ground under the big tree."

The student looked under the tree and started to move the soil away. Before long he found a bottle. When he held it up to the light he saw there was something inside the bottle. It was jumping up and down like a frog.

■tire ~ out ~を疲れさせる　■get an idea of ~を知る　■call out 叫ぶ　■over here こっちに　■soil 图土　■hold ~ up to the light ~を光にかざす

瓶のなかのお化け

「どこに行くんだね、息子よ。休まないと、へとへとになるぞ」

「遠くには行かないよ、お父さん。森のなかで鳥や木々に囲まれているのが気持ちいいだけだから」

息子がもう少し歩いていくと、古い大きな木のところに来た。木のまわりを歩いて、どれくらいの大きさか調べようとした。

「なあ、古い木よ。たくさんの鳥がおまえの枝に巣を作っているね」息子は静かに語りかけ、木を見上げた。

そのとき、声が聞こえた気がした。息子が真剣に耳をそばだてると、声はこんなことを言った。「出してくれ！ 出してくれ！」

あたりを見回しても何も見えなかったので、息子は叫んだ。「どこにいるんだい？ 姿が見えないぞ」

「こっちだ」声が答えた。「大きな木の下の地面のなかだ」

学生は木の下をのぞいて、土をどかしはじめた。まもなく、瓶を見つけた。瓶を光にかざすと、なかに何か入っているのが見えた。それはカエルのようにぴょんぴょんと跳びはねていた。

The Bottled Spirit

"Let me out! Let me out!" it cried again. The student felt sorry for it. He took out the stopper. As soon as he did so a spirit came out of the bottle. It grew and grew until it was almost half the size of the tree. It looked down at the student below it.

"Do you know," asked the spirit in a deep, low voice, "what you will get for letting me out of the bottle?"

"No," replied the student fearlessly, "How could I know?"

"I must break your neck!" answered the spirit.

"I'm sorry that you didn't tell me that before I let you out. But you will have to wait. There are other people we must talk to before you can break my neck."

"People or no people, I must break your neck. When I was put in the bottle I had to promise that if I ever escaped I would break the neck of whoever let me out."

"Oh well," replied the student coolly, "if you must, you must. But first you must prove to me, that it was really you who sat in the bottle. If you can get in the bottle again I will be sure it was you. Then you can do what you like with me."

■feel sorry 気の毒に思う　■stopper 图栓　■fearlessly 副恐れずに　■A or no A Aなどどうでもいい　■if someone ever もし〜なら　■prove 動証明する

瓶のなかのお化け

「出してくれ！ 出してくれ！」と、怒鳴り声がふたたび聞こえた。学生は気の毒になって、栓を抜いてやった。その途端、お化けが瓶から出てきた。どんどんと大きくなり、木のほぼ半分の高さにまでなった。お化けは学生を見下ろした。

「知っているか」お化けが深く低い声でたずねた。「おれを瓶から出したお礼に何をもらえるのか？」

「知らないよ」学生が恐れずに答えた。「知っているわけがないだろう？」

「おれは、おまえの首をへし折らねばならん」お化けが答えた。

「あんたを出す前に言ってくれればよかったのにな。しかし、ちょっと待ってくれないか。ぼくの首を折るのは、ほかの人たちの意見も聞いてからにしてくれ」

「ほかの者など、ほうっておけ。おまえの首をへし折らねばならん。おれが瓶に入れられたとき、瓶から出られたら、だれであれ、出してくれた者の首を折ると約束させられたからな」

「ああ、そうかい」学生が平然として答えた。「そうしなければいけないのなら、すればいいさ。でも、その前にぼくに証明してくれないか。瓶のなかに座っていたのが、本当にあんただってことをね。もう一度、瓶のなかに入れるのなら、あんただってことがわかる。そのあとで、ぼくを好きなようにすればいいだろう」

The Bottled Spirit

The spirit said it was easy to get back into the bottle. He got smaller and smaller until he was able to get back into the bottle. As soon as the spirit was in the bottle the student pushed the stopper back in.

As soon as he realized what had happened the spirit began to shout, "Let me out! Oh please, let me out!" The student put the bottle on the forest floor and began to walk away.

"Come back, please! If you let me out I will give you something that will make you rich for the rest of your life."

"How do I know that you are not trying to fool me?" replied the student.

"I promise I will not hurt you in any way if you let me out. If you don't let me out you will miss a chance to be happy forever."

The student thought a long time and then decided to take the chance. He removed the stopper and once again the spirit grew bigger and bigger until the student could hardly see the sky.

■get back 戻る　■floor 图地面　■fool 動だます　■walk away 立ち去る　■rest of life 一生　■in any way 決して　■take a chance いちかばちかやってみる

瓶のなかのお化け

　お化けは、瓶のなかに戻るなんて簡単だと言った。そして、どんどん小さくなり、とうとう瓶のなかに入れるくらいになった。お化けが瓶に入った途端、学生は栓を閉めた。

　お化けは何が起こったかわかった途端、叫び出した。「出してくれ！ なあ、頼むから、出してくれ！」。学生は瓶を森の地面にほうり出したまま、歩きはじめた。

「戻ってくれ、お願いだ！ おれを出してくれたら、いい物をあげるから。それがあれば、おまえはこれからずっと金持ちでいられるぞ」

「あんたがぼくをだまそうとしていないか、どうしてわかる？」学生が答えた。
「出してくれたら、おまえを決して傷つけないと約束する。出してくれなかったら、おまえは幸せになる機会を永遠に失うことになる」

　学生は長いあいだ考えたが、運に任せてやってみることにした。栓を抜くと、またもや、お化けはどんどん大きくなり、ほとんど空が見えなくなった。

The Bottled Spirit

"Now I will do as I promised," said the spirit. He gave the student a magic wand and said, "If someone is in pain, and you touch the place it hurts with one end of this wand, they will get better. If you touch something made of iron with the other end of the wand, the iron will be turned into silver."

"Here, let me try it," said the student. He took the wand and went over to a tree that had a piece cut out of it and touched it. Straight away the cut was replaced and the tree looked healthy and strong. "It really is a magic wand. You have done as you promised."

The student and the spirit thanked each other and said good-bye.

When the student returned to his father, the old man asked him where he had been for such a long time. "I knew you would never make it as a woodcutter," he said sadly.

"Don't be upset father; I will soon make everything right."

■in pain 痛みを感じて　■end of 〜の先端　■get better よくなる　■straight away たちまち　■replace 勵元に戻す　■make it as 〜として成功する

瓶のなかのお化け

「さあ、約束通りお礼をやるぞ」お化けが言った。そして、学生に魔法の杖をわたして言った。「だれかが痛みを訴えたら、杖のこっちの端で痛むところに触れるんだ。そうすれば、よくなるからな。もう一方の端で、鉄でできたものに触れると、鉄は銀に変わる」

「ここで、試してみよう」と学生が言い、杖を持って1本の木に近づいた。その木は一部分が切り取られていた。杖の端でその木に触れると、たちまち切り取られた部分が元通りになり、木は丈夫で強そうになった。「本当に魔法の杖だ。約束を守ってくれたんだね」

学生とお化けは互いに礼を言って、別れた。

学生が父親のところに戻ると、老人は、こんなに長いあいだどこをうろついていたんだとたずね、「おまえが木こりなんかになれっこないことは、わかっていたさ」と悲しそうに言った。

「悲しまないで、お父さん。もうすぐ何事もうまくいくようになるからね」

The Bottled Spirit

The son picked up his ax and touched it with the wand. "I'll cut down this tree with one blow," he said and gave the tree a mighty hit. However, because the ax was now made of silver it nearly broke.

"What have you done?" shouted the father. "We cannot return this ax to our neighbor. We'll have to buy a new one. But, what can we buy a new ax with? We have no money."

"Father, it's not so bad," said the son, "I can pay for the ax."

"You fool! How can you pay for the ax? You have no money. I should never have let you come woodcutting."

The son waited a while then said, "Father, I can't work any more today. Let's take the rest of the day off."

"You aren't thinking straight, you young fool. Even if you don't want to work, I must work. If I don't work, we will have nothing to eat tonight. You go home. You are no use in the forest anyway."

"I can't find my way home alone. It's my first time in the forest. Come with me please."

■blow 名一撃 ■mighty 形強力な ■pay for 〜の代価を払う ■day off（平日に取る）休み ■not think straight どうかしている ■even if たとえ〜だとしても

瓶のなかのお化け

　息子は斧を持ち上げて、杖で触れた。「一振りで、この木を切ってみせるから」と息子は言って、力一杯、木を打った。けれども、斧は銀に変わっていたので、ほとんど壊れてしまった。

　「何をしたんだ？」父親が叫んだ。「もう、お隣に斧を返せなくなったじゃないか。新しい物を買わなきゃならんが、どうやって買うというんだ？　一文無しだというのに」

　「お父さん、そんなに心配することはないよ」息子が言った。「ぼくが斧のお金を払うよ」
　「ばか者め！　どうやって斧のお金を払えるんだ？　おまえは一文無しだぞ。木を切りにつれて来るんじゃなかった」
　息子はしばらく待って言った。「お父さん、ぼくはもう今日は働けないよ。このへんで帰ろうよ」
　「まともに考えることもできないのか、愚か者め。おまえが働きたくなくても、わしは働かなきゃならん。そうしないと、今晩、食べる物が何もないのだ。おまえは家に帰れ。森にいても、どうせ、何の役にも立たんからな」
　「ひとりじゃ道がわからないよ。森に来たのははじめてだからね。いっしょに帰ってほしいんだ」

The Bottled Spirit

The father became less angry and after a few more words he took his son home. When they were near their house the father sent his son to the market to try and sell the broken ax. "Get a good price, for I will have to save money to buy a new one."

The son went to the silver shop in town. When the owner of the shop measured the weight of the ax he said, "This is worth four hundred dollars. But now, I only have three hundred dollars. I will pay you the other hundred when I get it next month."

The son was very happy. When he arrived home he said, "Father, I have some money. Tell me how much a new ax costs."

"One dollar," replied the father.

"Well, give our neighbor two dollars, I'm sure he'll be happy with that. I have a lot of money. Here, take this," said the son, handing over one hundred dollars. "You shall always have everything you want."

■save money お金を貯める　■measure 動 測定する　■worth 形 ～相当の　■hand over 手渡す

瓶のなかのお化け

　父親は怒りもかなり収まったので、もう少し文句を言ったあと、息子と家に帰ることにした。家が近づくと、父親は息子を市場にやり、壊れた斧を売らせようとした。「いい値で売るんだ。お金を貯めて、新しいのを買わなきゃならんからな」

　息子は、町の銀細工の店に行った。店主は斧の重さを測ると言った。「これは400ドルの値打ちがあります。ところが、ここには300ドルしかありません。残りの100ドルは来月支払うことにします」

　息子はとても喜び、家に着くと言った。「お父さん。お金をいくらか手に入れましたよ。新しい斧はいくらですか？」

「1ドルだ」父親が答えた。
「それでは、お隣に2ドルあげてください。きっと喜んでくれますよ。お金がたくさんあるんです。さあ、これを受け取ってください」息子はそう言うと、父親に100ドル以上わたした。「ほしい物はいつでも何でも買えますよ」

The Bottled Spirit

"Goodness me," cried the old man, "where did all this money come from?"

The father could hardly believe it when the student told him the story of the bottled spirit.

After a while, the father got used to not working anymore. The son used the rest of the money to finish college. Once again, his teachers were pleased with his work. In time, because his wand could heal all illnesses, the student became the most famous doctor in the world.

■goodness me 何てことだ　■get used to ～になじむ　■be pleased with ～に喜んでいる　■in time やがて　■heal 動 ～を治す

瓶のなかのお化け

「何とまあ」父親が叫んだ。「こんなお金をどこで手に入れたんだい？」

　父親は、学生から瓶のなかのお化けの話を聞いても、ほとんど信じられなかった。

　しばらくすると、父親は働かなくてもいい暮らしに慣れてきた。息子は残りのお金を使って大学を終了した。またもや、先生たちは学生が優秀な成績を修めたことを喜んだ。学生は魔法の杖でどんな病気も治すことができたので、やがて世界で一番名高い医者になった。

The Three Spinning Women

Once upon a time, there was a girl who would not work. She was supposed to work at the spinning wheel making thread. One day her mother got very angry and began hitting her. "Oh, why won't you work like other girls?" the mother yelled.

The queen, who happened to be passing, heard the yelling and she went into the house. She asked the mother why she was hitting her daughter. The woman did not want to say it was because her daughter would not work, so she said, "I cannot get her away from the spinning wheel, and I am poor and cannot buy the material she needs to make thread."

■spin 動糸を紡ぐ　■spinning wheel 糸車　■thread 名糸　■yell 動怒鳴る
■happen to たまたま〜する　■pass 動（道などを）通る

糸を紡ぐ三人の女

　むかしむかし、働くのがいやな娘がいた。娘の仕事は糸車で糸を紡ぐことだった。ある日、母親がかんかんに怒って、娘をたたきはじめた。「まったく、どうしてほかの娘のように働かないんだい？」母親が怒鳴った。

　たまたまそこを通りかかったお后が、怒鳴り声を聞きつけ、その家のなかに入った。お后は母親に、どうして娘をたたくのかたずねた。母親は、娘が働かないからだとは言いたくなかったので、こう答えた。「娘は糸を紡ぐのが好きで、糸車から離れようとしないからです。おまけに貧しくて、娘に糸を紡ぐ材料を買ってやれません」

The Three Spinning Women

The queen said, "Perhaps I can help you, I have a lot of material at the palace. I would love it if your daughter came along and worked for me."

Of course the mother agreed to this. When they arrived at the palace the queen showed the daughter three rooms. They were all large rooms, and they were all full of material waiting to be turned into thread.

"Here you are, my dear, if you spin all this into thread you can marry my oldest son."

The girl was left alone and quickly started to cry. She knew that even if she worked for a hundred years she would not finish the job the queen had given her.

For three days she cried and she wondered what the queen would say when she found out that she was not working. She went to the window and thought sadly of her family. Looking down, she saw three old women outside the palace. One had a large right foot, one had a mouth twice the usual size, and the third had one arm bigger than any man's.

■perhaps 副 たぶん　■would love ぜひとも〜を望む　■come along 同行する
■turn into 〜に変わる　■wonder 動 〜かしらと思う

糸を紡ぐ三人の女

　お后が言った。「わたくしが助けてあげられそうですよ。城にはたくさんの材料があります。あなたの娘さんが城に来て、わたくしのために働いてくれないものかしらね」
　もちろん、母親は承知した。城に着くと、お后は娘に3つの部屋を見せた。どれも大きな部屋で、どの部屋も糸に紡ぐ材料で溢れていた。

　「さあここですよ。ここにある材料をすべて紡いで糸にすれば、わたくしの長男と結婚させてあげますよ」
　娘はひとりになると、すぐに泣き出した。たとえ百年働いても、お后が与えた仕事を終わらせることなどできないことを知っていたからだ。

　3日のあいだ娘は泣き続け、何も仕事をしていないのをお后に見られたら、何と言われるかしらと思った。娘は窓辺に行き、家族のことを悲しく思い出した。見下ろすと、城の外に3人の老女が見えた。1人目は右足が大きく、2人目は口がふつうの2倍の大きさで、3人目は片腕が男の人よりも太かった。

The Three Spinning Women

The old women saw that the girl was upset and asked her what the problem was. She told them and they said, "If you ask us to your wedding and tell everybody we are your aunts, we will do all the work for you."

"I will, of course I will," said the young girl happily.

She let in the three strange-looking old women and they began to spin. The girl did not let the queen know about the three women, and the queen was very pleased at the amount of thread being made.

Soon all the material had been spun into thread. As the three strange women left the palace, one of them said to the girl "Remember your promise to us. Ask us to come when you get married and you will have great happiness."

When the girl showed the queen the empty rooms the queen was so happy that she set the date for the marriage right away.

The girl said, "I would like my three aunts to come on the marriage day. They are three old women but they have been very kind to me. If you will allow it I would like them to share our table."

■amount 图総量　■spun 動spin（紡ぐ）の過去分詞　■set the date for ～の日取りを決める　■marriage 图結婚（式）

糸を紡ぐ三人の女

　老女たちは娘が悲しそうにしているのを見て、何を悩んでいるのとたずねた。娘が打ち明けると、老女たちが言った。「あんたが、わたしたちを結婚式に呼んでくれて、わたしたちを伯母さんだとみんなに紹介してくれたら、あんたの仕事を全部やってあげるよ」
　「もちろん、そうしますとも」娘はうれしそうに答えた。
　奇妙な姿をした３人の老女たちは娘に部屋に通されると、糸を紡ぎはじめた。娘は老女たちのことを、お后には知られないようにした。お后は糸がたくさん紡がれるのを見ると、とても喜んだ。

　まもなく、材料すべてが紡がれて、糸になった。３人の奇妙な老女が城を去るとき、ひとりが娘に言った。「わたしたちとの約束を忘れないでおくれ。結婚式にわたしたちを招待してくれたら、大きな幸せが手に入るよ」
　娘がお后に空になった部屋を見せると、お后はたいへん喜び、すぐに婚礼の日を決めた。

　娘が言った。「結婚式の日には、３人の伯母に来てもらいたいのです。みんな年を取っていますが、わたしにとても親切にしてくれました。お許しいただければ、伯母たちにわたしたちのテーブルに座ってもらいたいのです」

The Three Spinning Women

The queen and the prince agreed. When the day came, the spinning women arrived and they looked very strange. The girl quickly welcomed them and said, "Come and sit at my table, my dear aunts, next to the prince and I."

When he saw them the prince was quite upset. "Why," he asked his wife, "are your aunts so strange-looking?" Then he turned to one and asked, "How come you have such a large foot?"

"From spinning the wheel," she said.

"And how come you have such a big mouth?" he said to the next.

"From wetting the material," the second woman said.

"And you," he said to the third. "Why is your right arm so big, when your left one is the usual size?"

"From holding the thread," she said.

"Well then," said the prince after thinking for a moment. "My beautiful wife will never touch a spinning wheel again, even though she is so good at it!"

■turn to ～の方を向く　■how come どうして　■wet 動 ～をなめて湿らせる　■even though たとえ～だとしても

糸を紡ぐ三人の女

　お后と王子は承知した。結婚式の日になると、糸紡ぎ女たちがやって来たが、相変わらずとても奇妙に見えた。娘はすぐに喜んで迎えて言った。「伯母様たち、わたしのテーブルに来て、王子とわたしの隣に座ってくださいな」

　王子は老女たちを見ると、ひどく驚いた。「どうして、」と花嫁にたずねた。「おまえの伯母さんたちはあんなに奇妙な姿をしているのだい？」。そう言うと、王子は伯母のひとりのほうを向いて訊いた。「どうしてそんなに足が大きいのですか？」

　「糸車を回すからです」その伯母が答えた。

　「それでは、どうしてそんなに口が大きいのですか？」王子は２人目にたずねた。

　「材料をなめるからです」２人目が答えた。

　「それでは、あなたは」王子は３人目にたずねた。「どうしてそんなに右腕が太いのですか？　左腕はふつうの太さなのに」

　「糸を持つからです」３人目が答えた。

　「そうすると」王子はしばらく考えて言った。「わたしの美しい花嫁は、もう二度と糸車をさわらなくていいということにしよう。それが、とても得意であってもね！」

覚えておきたい英語表現

> it was only *the iron rings breaking from Henry's heart.*
> （p. 62, 15行目）
> ヘンリーが胸に巻いていた鉄の帯が外れたのだった。

　この「鉄の帯が外れる」という表現は、ドイツ語のことわざである「Mir fällt ein Stein vom Herzen」に掛けた言葉です。直訳は「心の石が落ちる」、つまり「（心配事などの）肩の荷が落ちる」という意味です。

　忠実な家来であるヘンリーの心配事が解決したことを暗示しています。王子が元の姿に戻り美しい姫と結ばれ、もちろんその美しい姫も幸福で、それを見たヘンリーも嬉しい——3人の幸福を意味しているので、鉄の輪が三つあるのです。グリム兄弟の「粋」を感じさせる物語の締め方と言えるでしょう。

　ちなみにこのThe Frog Princeは第1版から第7版まで一貫して巻頭に置かれていることからも、この物語に対するグリム兄弟の思い入れを感じることができます。

> He looked around but could see *nothing* ～ （p. 68, 13行目）
> 彼はあたりを見回したが何も見ることができなかった。

　nothingは「何も～ない」という意味の代名詞です。could see（見ることができた）/ nothing（何もない）つまり「何も見えなかった」と意訳することは比較的簡単です。しかしこれを英会話で使いこなすことは、日本人学習者にとってハードルが高いです。通常の日本語には、否定の言葉を目的語にする表現がないからです。例文で覚えましょう。

【例文】

I had *nothing* to do.
何もすることがなかった（暇だった）。

It was *nothing.*
何でもなかったよ。
　＊どうしたの？ 何かあったの？ と問われた時などへの返事として。

I know *nothing* at all.
まったく存じません。

I knew you would never *make it* as a wood cutter. (p. 74, 16行目)
お前が木こりになんかなれっこないだろうってことは分かっていたのに。

---

　make itはとても便利な表現です。ぜひ使いこなしていただきたいと思って取り上げました。makeはよくご存じの「作る」ですね。人の手で何かを作るという原義から、「なんとか頑張って〜する」というニュアンスが導き出されます。itは状況全般を指します。make itには「時間に間に合う」「成功する」「時間の都合をつける」「困難を乗り切る」など多くの使い方があります。ぜひ口語でたくさん使っていただきたい表現です。

【例文】

I could *make it* to the bus in time.
なんとかバスに間に合ったよ。

You can *make it*!
君ならできるよ！

I won't be able to *make it* to the meeting.
会議には出席できそうにもないよ。

We could *make it* through the typhoon.
無事に台風をやりすごしたよ。

　いずれもmakeの「なんとか頑張って〜する」が、話し手の気持ちに込められていることを感じ取ってください。

覚えておきたい英語表現

> there was a girl who *would not* work. （p. 82, 1行目）
> どうしても働こうとしない女の子がいました。

　wouldは助動詞willの過去形です。「〜だろう」という意味以外にもうひとつ覚えておくべき意味があります。それは「どうしても〜しようとする（肯定文）」「どうしても〜しようとはしなかった（否定文）」という「固執」の用法です。

　　　　She *would* go there anyway.
　　　　彼女はどうしてもそこへ行くと言いはった。

　　　　He *wouldn't* say yes.
　　　　彼はどうしてもYESと言おうとしなかった。
　　　　＊固執の用法ではI'dのように短縮しません。wouldを強めに発音して強調します。

　この話は童話や民話には珍しく、怠け者が怠け者のまま幸せになる話です。きっと日本の落語のように、オチで人を笑わせるお話だと思われます。童話集に載るほど語り継がれた話ですから、大傑作の笑い話だったはずです。今ほど娯楽がなかった時代のドイツの人々が、この話を聞いてお腹を抱えて笑い転げていた姿を想像してみてください。

Part 3

The Shoes That Were Danced Full of Holes
踊ってぼろぼろになった靴

The Fisherman and His Wife
漁師とおかみさん

The Shoes That Were Danced Full of Holes

Once upon a time there was a king who had twelve beautiful daughters. They slept together in a long room and their beds stood close together in a row. Each night the king would shut the bedroom door so that no one could get in or out.

In the morning, however, when he opened the door, it was always the same. The girls' shoes had been danced full of holes. No one knew how this could happen. The girls always said that they had slept soundly through the night.

■full of 〜でいっぱいである　■close together くっついて　■in a row 一列に並んで
■get in or out 出入りする

踊ってぼろぼろになった靴

　むかしむかし、王様がいた。王様には12人の美しい娘がいた。娘たちは細長い部屋でいっしょに眠り、ベッドはぴったりと1列に並んでいた。毎晩、王様は娘たちの寝室の戸に鍵をかけ、だれも出入りできないようにした。

　ところが、朝になり、王様が戸をあけると、いつも同じことが起こっていた。姫たちの靴が踊って穴だらけになっていたのだ。どうしてそうなるのか、だれにもわからなかった。姫たちはいつも、一晩じゅう、ぐっすり眠っていたと言った。

The Shoes That Were Danced Full of Holes

The king could not find out what happened. He decided to find someone who could find out what happened. The king made an announcement to everyone in the country. Whoever could find out how the shoes were danced full of holes could marry one of his daughters. The man could be the next king. However, anyone who tried but was not successful in three days, would have his head cut off.

Soon a young prince became the first to try and find the answer. The king was very nice to him and made him feel most welcome. A bed was put in the hall near the princesses' room for him. At night, the prince lay outside waiting to see what happened.

After a little while, however, his eyes began to feel very heavy and soon he was asleep. When he awoke in the morning it was clear that the twelve sisters had been to a dance. There were holes in all their shoes. The second and third nights the prince failed again. On the fourth morning, his head was cut off.

Other princes and lords came and tried to find the answer. All of them fell asleep and all of them lost their heads.

■announcement 名告知　■cut off 切り落とす　■fail 動失敗する　■lord 名貴族

踊ってぼろぼろになった靴

　王様は何があったのかわからなかったので、それを突き止めてくれる人を探すことにした。王様は国じゅうにおふれを出した。どうして靴が踊って穴だらけになったのか突き止めた者はだれでも、娘のひとりと結婚できるというのだ。その上、次の王様になれるという。ところが、名乗り出て、3日以内に答えを見つけ出せないと、だれであっても首をはねられるということだった。

　ほどなく、若い王子が最初に名乗りを上げ、答えを見つけようとした。王様はその王子にとても親切で、大歓迎をした。ベッドが、姫たちの寝室の隣にある控えの間に置かれた。夜になると、王子は姫たちの寝室の外で横になり、何が起こるか待ちかまえた。

　ところが、まもなくすると、王子のまぶたがとても重くなりはじめ、すぐに眠ってしまった。朝になって目覚めると、12人の姉妹が踊りにいっていたのは明らかだった。どの靴も穴があいていたからだ。2日目の晩も3日目の晩も、王子は失敗を繰り返した。それで、4日目の朝に首をはねられてしまった。

　ほかにも王子や貴族たちがやって来て、答えを見つけようとしたが、だれもが眠ってしまい、首をはねられた。

The Shoes That Were Danced Full of Holes

One day, a poor soldier came to the city. When an old woman asked him why he had come, he laughed and said, "Maybe, I will try and find out what happens at night in the princesses' bedroom. If I succeed I will be the next king. Not a bad price for three nights' work."

Although he probably had not meant what he said the old woman believed him. She quickly said, "It is not so difficult. Do not drink the wine they bring you at night. Pretend to drink it and pretend to fall asleep." Then she gave the poor soldier an old coat. "If you throw this over yourself no one will be able to see you. Then you can follow the twelve girls and see where they go."

The soldier went to the king and offered to find the answer to the problem. Even though he was not a lord or prince, the king was kind to him and wished him good luck.

■soldier 名兵隊　■price 名代価　■pretend to 〜するふりをする　■throw 〜 over 〜をサッとはおる　■wish someone good luck (人) に幸運を祈る

踊ってぼろぼろになった靴

　ある日、貧しい兵隊がその町にやって来た。おばあさんに、どうしてやって来たのかとたずねられると、兵隊は笑って言った。「お姫様の寝室で夜に何が起こっているのか突き止めてみるためかな。成功したら、次の王様だ。3晩の仕事にしたら、割の悪い話じゃないからな」

　兵隊はおそらく本気で言ったわけではなかっただろうが、おばあさんは、それをうのみにした。それで、すぐに言った。「そんなに難しいことじゃないよ。お姫様たちが夜にあんたのところに持って来るワインを飲むんじゃないよ。飲んだふりをして、眠ったふりをするんだよ」。それから、兵隊に古い上着をわたした。「これをかぶると、だれにもあんたの姿が見えなくなる。そうすれば、12人のお姫様のあとをつけて、どこに行くのか確かめることができるよ」
　兵隊は王様の前に行き、問題の答えを見つけたいと申し出た。兵隊は貴族でも王子でもなかったが、王様は親切で、幸運を祈ってくれた。

The Shoes That Were Danced Full of Holes

At bedtime, the soldier was led to the hall outside the girls' room. When he was getting into bed, the oldest princess brought him a glass of wine. When she was not looking, he quickly poured the wine on the ground behind. Then he held the glass to his mouth like he had drunk it. He then lay down and after a few minutes began to breathe heavily as if he were sleeping.

The twelve princesses heard his snores and the oldest said, "He, too, could have saved himself trouble, and his life!"

Then the princesses got up and put on their best clothes. They laughed and sang and thought about the dancing they were going to do.

The youngest princess seemed a little unhappy and said, "I don't feel good about this evening. Something will go wrong, I can feel it."

"Don't be a fool," said the oldest princess, "what is there to be afraid of? Remember all the princes who tried to find out what we do at night. How could this poor soldier do any better? I gave him the wine. He won't wake up before morning."

■bedtime 名就寝時間　■pour 動（液体を）流す　■snore 名いびき　■go wrong 悪い方向に進む

踊ってぼろぼろになった靴

　床につく時刻になると、兵隊は姫たちの部屋の隣にある控えの間に案内された。ベッドに入ろうとしていると、一番上の姫がグラス一杯のワインを持って来た。姫が見ていないすきに、兵隊はうしろの床に、すばやくワインを流した。そして、グラスを口元に当て、飲んだように見せた。そのあと横になり、数分後に深い呼吸をして、眠っているように見せかけた。

　12人の姫たちは兵隊のいびきを聞くと、一番上の姫が言った。「この人も、こんなことに手を出さなければ、命をなくさずにすんだものを！」

　そのあと、姫たちは起き上がり、一番上等の服を着た。笑って歌いながら、これから踊りにいくのを心待ちにした。

　一番末の姫だけは少し不安そうに見え、こう言った。「今夜はいやな予感がする。何か悪いことが起こるわ。それを感じるもの」

　「ばかなことを言うんじゃないの」一番上の姫が言った。「何を恐れることがあるの？　どの王子も、わたしたちが夜に何をしているか突き止めようとしても、できなかったのよ。こんな貧しい兵隊がもっとうまくやれるわけがないわ。それに、ワインを飲ませたから、朝まで起きやしないわ」

The Shoes That Were Danced Full of Holes

Before they left, the princesses looked at the soldier again. He seemed to be asleep. The oldest daughter went to the head of her bed and hit it. The floor opened up in a secret opening and the girls went down through the opening. The soldier, who had been watching them, put on his magic coat and followed close behind the youngest princess. He got too close, however, and stepped on her dress. She shouted, "Who is that? Someone stepped on my dress."

"There's no one there," said the oldest, "you must have caught it on something." The princesses continued down the stairs to the bottom. In front of them was a small forest of beautiful trees. A winding road went through the forest. The girls went into the forest. The soldier thought he might have to prove what had happened so he broke a branch off a tree. The youngest princess heard it and said, "What was that? Didn't you hear a noise?"

"It was one of our princes firing a gun to welcome us," said the oldest princess.

■open up 開く　■opening 穴、通路　■get close 接近する　■step on ～を踏みつける　■winding 曲がりくねった　■break off 折り取る　■fire a gun 発砲する

踊ってぼろぼろになった靴

　出かける前に、姫たちはもう一度、兵隊を見つめた。兵隊は眠っているように見えた。一番上の姫が自分のベッドの頭板まで行き、とんとんとたたいた。すると床が開いて秘密の通路が現われ、姫たちは通路を降りていった。これを見ていた兵隊は、魔法の上着を着て、末の姫のすぐうしろから、ついていった。ところが、あまりに近づきすぎたので、姫の服を踏んでしまった。姫は叫んだ。「だれなの？　だれかがわたしの服を踏んだわ」

　「だれもいないわよ」一番上の姫が言い返した。「きっと、何かに引っかかったのよ」。姫たちは階段を降り続け、底に着いた。目の前には美しい木が広がる小さな森があり、1本の曲がりくねった道が、森を抜けていた。姫たちは森のなかに入っていった。兵隊は、何が起こったか証明する物があったほうがいいと考え、木から枝を1本折った。末の姫がその音を聞いて言った。「あれは何なの？　姉さんたち、あの音が聞こえなかった？」

　「あれは王子のひとりが、わたしたちを迎えるために祝砲を撃っている音よ」一番上の姫が言った。

The Shoes That Were Danced Full of Holes

The princesses continued down the road and soon came to a lake. There were twelve boats on the shore. Next to each boat stood a tall prince. The princes and princesses paired off and each pair got into a boat. The soldier quickly got into the boat with the youngest princess. After a while her prince said, "Why does the boat seem so much heavier than usual? I can barely move it tonight."

"It must be the weather," replied the youngest princess, "it's so hot I can hardly breathe."

On the other side of the lake was a beautiful palace. There were bright lights everywhere and the sound of music could be heard across the water. The boats landed and the princes and the princesses entered the palace. They started dancing and the soldier watched them. The youngest princess stopped to drink some wine, but the soldier drank it from her glass before she could drink it.

■pair off ペアになる　■barely 副 どうにかこうにか〜する　■breathe 動 息をする
■land 動 上陸する

踊ってぼろぼろになった靴

　姫たちが歩き続けると、まもなく湖に出た。岸には小舟が12艘あり、それぞれの小舟の隣には背の高い王子たちが立っていた。王子と姫は2人ずつ組になり、舟に乗った。兵隊は素早く末の姫の舟に乗り込んだ。しばらくすると、姫の相手の王子が言った。「どうして舟が、いつもよりひどく重く感じるのだろう？　今夜はとても漕ぎづらいな」

　「きっとお天気のせいよ」末の姫が答えた。「とっても暑くて、息もできないくらいだわ」

　湖の向こうには、美しい城が建っていた。あちこちに明るい光が輝き、そこから音楽が響いてきた。舟が着くと、王子と姫たちは城に入った。みんなが踊りはじめると、兵隊はじっと見つめた。末の姫が立ち止まってワインを飲もうとしたが、兵隊は姫が飲む前に、姫のグラスから飲んでしまった。

The Shoes That Were Danced Full of Holes

The youngest princess was surprised and afraid. Again her older sisters told her everything was okay. They danced until three o'clock in the morning. By then their shoes were full of holes and they could dance no more.

As they were going home the soldier quietly moved ahead of them and arrived home before them. When the princesses got home he was back in bed and he looked like he had never moved.

The next morning, the soldier said nothing. He watched the same thing happen on the second and third nights. To help prove his story he took a glass from the palace and some water from the lake.

On the fourth morning, he put the branch, and the glass and water under his coat and went to the king.

The king asked, "Where do my daughters dance their shoes full of holes each night?"

■okay 形 問題なく、大丈夫で　■ahead of 〜より先んじて　■get home 帰宅する

踊ってぼろぼろになった靴

　末の姫は驚いて怯えたが、またもや、年上の姫たちが何も心配はいらないと言い聞かせた。みんなは明けがたの3時まで踊り続けた。そのころには姫たちの靴は穴だらけで、これ以上、踊ることはできなかった。

　姫たちが家に帰ろうとすると、兵隊は音を立てずに姫たちの前を行き、先に家に着いた。姫たちが家に着くころには、兵隊はベッドに戻っていて、ずっとそこにいたように見えた。

　次の朝が来ても、兵隊は昨夜のことは何も話さなかった。2日目の晩にも3日目の晩にも、同じことが起こるのを目撃した。自分の話を証明するために、兵隊は城からはグラスをひとつ、湖からは水を少し持ち帰った。

　4日目の朝、兵隊は、枝、グラス、それに水を上着の下に隠して、王様の前に行った。
　王様がたずねた。「わたしの娘たちは、毎晩いったいどこで、靴がぼろぼろになるまで踊っているのだ？」

The Shoes That Were Danced Full of Holes

The soldier said:

"In an underground palace, across a lake, with twelve princes." He showed the king the branch, glass, and water and told him the full story.

The king called for his daughters. He asked them if the soldier was telling the truth. The girls saw the glass and the branch from the beautiful forest and they knew the soldier knew their secret.

Then the king said "Which of my daughters do you want to marry?"

"I am not so very young," said the soldier, "I will marry the oldest one."

They married and soon after the soldier became the next king.

■underground 形 地下の　■ask someone if 〜かどうかを（人に）尋ねる　■soon after 〜からまもなく

踊ってぼろぼろになった靴

　兵隊が答えた。
　「湖の向こうの地下の城で、12人の王子たちと」。兵隊は王様に、枝やグラス、それに水を見せて、一部始終を話した。

　王様は姫たちを呼び出し、兵隊の言ったことは本当かとたずねた。姫たちはグラスと美しい森で折られた枝を見て、兵隊に自分たちの秘密を知られたと悟った。

　それから王様が兵隊に訊いた。「どの娘と結婚したいかね？」

　「わたしはそんなに若くはありません」兵隊が言った。「ですから、一番上の姫と結婚させてください」
　2人は結婚し、まもなく兵隊は次の王様になった。

The Fisherman and His Wife

There was once a fisherman who lived with his wife close to the sea. Their house was very old, and the rooms were small and dark. The woman found it very unpleasant to live there and wanted to move somewhere nicer, but they did not have the money.

One day, when he was fishing, the fisherman pulled in his line and on the end was the biggest fish he had ever caught. To his surprise the fish started talking, "Listen fisherman," he said, "please don't kill me for I am not really a fish, I am a magic prince. You would not enjoy it if you ate me, so put me back in the water."

■fisherman 名漁師　■pull in 釣り上げる　■line 名釣り糸　■end 名（糸などの）先

漁師とおかみさん

　むかしむかし、漁師が、おかみさんと海のそばに住んでいた。2人の家はとても古く、部屋は狭くて暗かった。おかみさんはそこに住むのを不愉快に思い、もっといいところに越したいと願っていた。けれども、お金がなかった。

　ある日、漁師が釣りをしていたとき、釣り糸を引くと、その先にこれまで釣ったこともない大きな魚がかかっていた。驚いたことに、その魚がしゃべり出した。「聞いてください、漁師さん」魚が言った。「どうか、わたしを殺さないで。わたしは本当の魚ではなく、魔法にかかった王子なのです。わたしを食べても、おいしくありませんよ。ですから、水に戻してください」

The Fisherman and His Wife

"Well," said the fisherman, "I wouldn't think of keeping a fish that could speak." He quickly put the fish back in the water and watched as it swam away in the clear, blue sea. He caught nothing else that day and went home to his wife in their old house.

"Have you not caught anything today, husband?"

"No," replied he, "I did catch one fish, a great big one, in fact, but he said he was a magic prince, so I let him go."

"You let him go, did you? I suppose you didn't ask for anything, did you?"

"No, I didn't. What should I have wished for?"

"You know I can't stand this old house, you should have asked him for a nice new one. Go back to the sea and call to him and tell him we want a new house. I'm sure he'll give us one."

The man did not really want to go, but he did not want to upset his wife either, so off he went to the sea.

When he reached the sea, he noticed that the waves were a little higher and the sea a darker blue. He went to the shore and said:

■think of 〜しようかと考える　■suppose 動 〜だと思う　■stand 動 〜を我慢する
■off he went　he went off（彼は出かけた）の倒置

漁師とおかみさん

「そうだな」漁師が言った。「わしも、話をする魚なんてほしくないからな」。そう言うと、すぐに魚を水に戻し、魚が透き通った青い海を泳いでいくのを見守った。漁師はその日はほかに何も釣れず、おかみさんの待つ古い家に帰った。

「今日は、何も釣れなかったのかい、あんた？」
「そうだ」亭主が答えた。「実は、魚を1匹、釣り上げた。すごく大きい奴だった。だけど、そいつは自分が魔法にかかった王子だと言ったから、逃がしてやったのさ」
「逃がしてやっただって？　あんた、何もお願いしなかったのかい？」
「ああ、そうだ。いったい何を願えばよかったんだ？」
「あんた、あたしがこの古い家に我慢がならないことを知っているだろう。きれいな新しい家をお願いすればよかったんだよ。海に戻って、魚を呼んで、新しい家をほしいと言っておいでよ。きっと、くれるはずだよ」

亭主は、あまり行きたくなかったが、おかみさんを怒らすのもいやだった。それで仕方なく、海に出かけた。
漁師が海に着くと、波が少し高くなり、海の色が前よりも暗い青になっていることに気づいた。漁師は岸に行って呼びかけた。

The Fisherman and His Wife

"Great fish in the sea, please listen to me,
 My wife won't let be, as I'd have it be."

When he had finished, the fish he had caught earlier came swimming up and said, "What does she want?"

"Well," said the man, "my wife thinks that because I let you go, I should have wished for something. I should have asked you for a new house as she does not like our old one."

"Go home," said the fish, "she has one already."

The man went home and found that in place of his old home was a new house. Indeed, everything in it was new: the kitchen, the bed, and they even had a little garden with all kinds of fruit trees. "This is much better," said his wife.

"Yes, we'll stay here and be very happy," replied the man.

"We'll see about that," said his wife quietly.

■let be 放っておく　■should have p.p. ～すべきだった　■as 腰 ～だから　■let ~ go ～を逃がす　■indeed 副本当に　■much better（～よりも）ずっといい　■see about ～について検討する

漁師とおかみさん

「海の大きな魚さん、どうか聞いとくれ。
　わしがいいと言っても、女房が言うことを聞かないんだ」

　漁師が言い終えると、先ほどつかまえた魚が泳いで来て、たずねた。「おかみさんは何がほしいというのだね？」
「やれやれ」漁師が言った。「女房は、わしがあんたを逃がしてやったのだから、何かお願いすればよかったと言うんだ。新しい家をお願いすればよかったとね。女房は今の古い家が気に入らないんだ」

「家にお帰り」魚が言った。「おかみさんは、もう新しい家を手に入れているよ」
　漁師が家に戻ると、古い家があったところに、新しい家が建っていた。それどころか、家のなかの物は、台所もベッドも、何もかもが新しかった。おまけに、小さな庭があり、そこにはあらゆる種類の果物の木があった。「前よりずっといいねえ」おかみさんが言った。
「そうだな。ここにいれば、とても幸せに暮らせそうだ」亭主が答えた。

「それはまあ考えてみないとね」おかみさんが静かに言った。

The Fisherman and His Wife

Everything was fine for the next two weeks but then the wife said, "Listen, husband, this new house is too small, far too small, and I need a bigger garden as well. Go back to the fish and tell him we want something bigger, like a nice, stone palace."

"No, wife," replied the fisherman, "the fish has already given us this house. I don't want to go to him again; he might be angry with me."

"Just go, will you? He will be happy to do it for the man who saved his life."

The man's heart was heavy, and he objected to going. He thought to himself that it wasn't right, but before long he found himself at the seashore looking at a sea that seemed almost angry. Nevertheless he called out to the fish:

"Great fish in the sea, please listen to me,
  My wife won't let be, as I'd have it be."

"Well, what does she want this time?" said the fish. "Oh," said the man a little fearfully, "she wants to live in a stone palace."

■object to ～を嫌う ■seashore 名 海辺 ■nevertheless 副 そうではあるものの

漁師とおかみさん

　それから2週間は何事もすばらしかったが、そのうちに、おかみさんが言い出した。「ねえ、あんた。この新しい家は狭すぎるよ。あんまりにも狭いよ。それにもっと大きな庭もほしいんだ。魚のところに行って、もっと大きい家がほしいと言っとくれ。立派な石の御殿のようなのをさ」

「だめだよ、おまえ」漁師が答えた。「魚はもう、この家をくれたじゃないか。また魚のところに行くのはいやだ。わしのことを怒るかもしれん」

「ちょっと行くだけのことじゃないか。命の恩人の言うことは喜んで聞いてくれるさ」
　漁師の心は重く、行きたくなかった。そんなことをするのは間違っていると思ったのだが、やがて気がつくと海辺にいた。海を見ると、まるで怒っているようだった。それでも、漁師は魚に呼びかけた。

「海の大きな魚さん、どうか聞いとくれ。
　　わしがいいと言っても、女房が言うことを聞かないんだ」

「それで今度は、おかみさんは何がほしいというのだね？」魚がたずねた。「いやはや」漁師は少しびくびくして言った。「女房は石の御殿に住みたいと言うんだ」

The Fisherman and His Wife

"Go home," said the fish, "she is standing in front of the door right now."

When the man arrived at the place where his house had been he found a great stone palace, and his smiling wife waiting on the steps.

"Well, aren't you coming in then," she said taking his arm. They entered the palace together. Their mouths dropped open in surprise. Everything was so beautiful. The walls were shiny and new, and there were beautiful, brightly colored things in every room. Behind the house was a large yard containing horses, dogs and many other farm animals; beyond the house was a great garden more than two miles long, filled with flowers, plants and beautiful trees.

"Well," said the wife, "Isn't this fine?"

"Yes," said the man, "and it shall remain so. We'll stay in this beautiful palace and be happy forever."

"We'll see about that," replied his wife quietly.

■step 名《-s》階段　■yard 名中庭　■contain 動～を収容する　■mile 名マイル《約1609.3m》　■remain 動～のままである

漁師とおかみさん

「家にお帰り」魚が言った。「おかみさんは、たった今、戸口に立っているよ」

亭主が家のあった場所に着くと、立派な石の御殿が建っていて、おかみさんがにこにこして、階段の上で待っていた。

「ねえ、なかに入ろうよ」おかみさんが亭主の腕を取って言った。2人はいっしょになかに入ると、驚きのあまり、口をあんぐりあけた。何もかもが、ひどく美しかった。壁は輝いていて新しく、どの部屋にもきれいな、明るい色をした物が置いてあった。家の裏には大きな中庭があり、馬や犬に、たくさんの家畜がいた。家の向こうには広大な庭があり、長さは2マイル以上で、花や植物、美しい木で一杯だった。

「ねえ」おかみさんが言った。「すてきじゃないの」

「そうだな」亭主が答えた。「ずっとこのままだといいな。このきれいな御殿にいれば、いつまでも幸せに暮らせそうだ」

「それはまあ考えてみないとね」おかみさんが静かに答えた。

The Fisherman and His Wife

The next morning the wife woke first. The sun had just risen and she could see the beautiful countryside out of her bedroom window. When she heard her husband waking up, she pushed him out of bed saying, "Come over here to the window. Look at this beautiful land. Why can't we be rulers of it? Go to the fish and tell him we want to be rulers of this land."

"Oh, wife!" said the man, "why should we be rulers? I don't want to be a ruler."

"Well, I do," shouted his wife, "now get to the fish and tell him to make us rulers."

The man went to the seashore. For the first time in his life he was afraid of the sea, for the waves were high and came rushing up the shore. Nevertheless he stood by the ocean and said:

"Great fish in the sea, please listen to me,
 My wife won't let be, as I'd have it be."

"What does she want this time?" said the fish.

■countryside 名田舎　■Come over here. こちらへいらっしゃい　■ruler 名支配者
■get to ～のところに行く　■nevertheless 副それにもかかわらず

漁師とおかみさん

　次の朝、おかみさんが先に目を覚ました。日が昇ったばかりで、寝室の窓から美しい田舎の景色が見えた。亭主が起きたことに気づくと、亭主をベッドから引っ張り出して言った。「窓のところに来て、この美しい地方をごらんよ。あたしたちで治められないものかね？　魚のところに行って、この地方の支配者になりたいって言っとくれ」

「何てことを、おまえ！」亭主が言った。「何でまた、わしらが支配者なんかになるんだ？　わしは、そんな者になりたくないよ」
　「でも、あたしはなりたいの」おかみさんが叫んだ。「さあ、魚のところに行って、あたしたちを支配者にしてほしいと頼んでおいでよ」
　亭主は海辺に行った。生まれてはじめて、海を怖いと思った。波が高く、岸に押し寄せていたのだ。それでも、亭主は岸に立ち、言った。

「海の大きな魚さん、どうか聞いとくれ。
　　わしがいいと言っても、女房が言うことを聞かないんだ」

「今度は、おかみさんは何がほしいと言うのだね？」魚がたずねた。

The Fisherman and His Wife

"Oh," said the man, almost as though he was talking to himself, "she wants to be ruler of our land."

"Go home," said the fish, "she has her wish."

The man went home, and as he got nearer to the stone palace he saw that it had got much larger. There were soldiers standing guard outside and servants running here and there. Inside, there were beautiful paintings on the walls, and almost everything seemed to be made of gold. The doors of the main hall opened into the biggest room he had ever seen.

In the middle of the room, with six ladies-in-waiting on either side of her, was his wife. She was seated high on a throne with a gold crown on her head. The fisherman went up to her and said "Well wife, you are ruler now."

"Yes," she replied, "I am."

He stood for a while looking at her and then said, "How great it is that you are ruler; now we won't wish for anything more."

"Not at all, husband," answered the wife and she became quite angry, "I'm getting tired of all this, and I can't stand it any longer. I must be queen of this country."

■as though まるで～するかのように　■painting 名絵画　■open into ～に通じる
■ladies-in-waiting 名侍女　■throne 名王座　■not at all ちっともそんなことはない

漁師とおかみさん

「いやはや」亭主はまるでひとりごとのように言った。「この地方の支配者になりたいと言うんだ」

「家にお帰り」魚が言った「おかみさんの望みはかなっているよ」

亭主は帰っていき、石の御殿に近づくと、前よりもっと大きくなっていることに気づいた。外では兵隊が見張りに立ち、家来があちこちを走り回っていた。家のなかでは、壁に美しい絵がかけられ、ほとんどの物が金でできているようだった。玄関広間の戸は、亭主が見たこともない大きな部屋に通じていた。

部屋のまんなかには、両側にそれぞれ6人の侍女を従えて、おかみさんがいた。王座に高く座り、金の冠をかぶっていた。漁師はおかみさんに近づいて言った。「おまえ、支配者になったのかい」

「そうよ」おかみさんが答えた。「支配者になったわ」

亭主は立って、しばらくおかみさんを見つめて言った。「支配者になるなんて、すごいじゃないか。もう、わしらには何も望むものはないな」

「そうはいかないよ、あんた」おかみさんは答えると、ひどく怒り出した。「こんなことにあきあきしたよ、もう我慢できそうにない。この国の女王にならなくちゃ気がすまないよ」

The Fisherman and His Wife

"Oh no, wife, not that. Why do you want to be queen, isn't this enough?"

His wife looked at him with her face set hard, "I want to be queen and I will be queen."

"But wife," cried the fisherman, "the fish, even though he is magic, cannot make you queen. There is only one queen in the country; the fish can't make you queen, I'm sure he can't."

"Don't say 'can't' to me, for I am a ruler, and you're only my husband. Now be off to the fish and get him to make me queen."

The man went off to the shore. He was unhappy and knew there was something wrong when he saw the sea. It was black and angry-looking and a great wind was driving the waves onto the shore. He stood by the edge and said:

"Great fish in the sea, please listen to me,
 My wife won't let be, as I'd have it be."

"What does she want?" asked the fish.

■be sure 間違いなく〜だと思う　■only 副 ほんの〜（でしかない）　■be off to 〜へ出かける　■drive 動 駆り立てる

漁師とおかみさん

「何を言うんだ、おまえ。それは無理だ。何でまた女王なんかになりたいんだ? これで十分じゃないか」

おかみさんは顔をこわばらせて、亭主を見つめた。「あたしが女王になりたいと言ったら、女王になるんだ」

「けれど、おまえ」漁師が叫んだ。「あの魚は魔法を使えても、おまえを女王にはできないよ。国には女王はひとりしかいないんだからな。あの魚はおまえを女王にできない。絶対にできっこない」

「あたしに、『できない』なんて、言わないでおくれ。あたしはこの地方の支配者で、あんたは、たかがあたしの亭主じゃないか。さあ、とっとと魚のところに行って、あたしを女王にしてと頼んでおくれ」

亭主は海辺に行った。心が沈み、海を見たときに何かおかしいと感じた。海はまっ黒で怒ったように見え、すさまじい風が波を岸に打ち上げていた。亭主は岸に立ち、言った。

「海の大きな魚さん、どうか聞いとくれ。
わしがいいと言っても、女房が言うことを聞かないんだ」

「おかみさんは何がほしいと言うのだね?」魚がたずねた。

The Fisherman and His Wife

"I am unhappy to say that she wants to be queen."

"Go home," said the fish, "she is queen already."

So the man went home and when he returned it looked as if the whole palace was made of gold. There were a great many soldiers, and hundreds of lords and ladies waiting in a beautiful room, which stretched as far as the eye could see. In the middle of the room, on a stand hundreds of feet high was a golden throne on which his wife sat.

When the man at last got close to her, he said, "Wife, are you queen now?"

"Yes," she replied, "I'm queen."

The man looked at her for a while and then he said, "How great it is that you are queen. It's hard to believe. You cannot possibly want anything else."

■stretch 動広がる　■stand 名壇　■cannot possibly do まさか〜できない

漁師とおかみさん

「こんなことを頼みたくないんだが、女王になりたいと言うんだ」

「家にお帰り」魚が言った。「おかみさんはもう女王になっているよ」

それで、亭主は帰っていき、戻ってみると宮殿全体が金でできているように見えた。大勢の兵隊がいて、数百人もの貴族や貴婦人が美しい部屋に控えていた。その部屋は見渡す限り広がっていた。部屋のまんなかには、金の玉座が数百フィートの高さの壇上にあり、そこにおかみさんが座っていた。

亭主はようやくおかみさんに近づくと、言った。「おまえ、女王になったのかい？」

「そうよ」おかみさんが答えた。「女王になったわ」

亭主はしばらくおかみさんを見つめて言った。「女王になるなんて、すごいじゃないか。とても信じられんよ。もう、なりたい者などないだろうな」

The Fisherman and His Wife

His wife just looked at him for a while but said nothing. The fisherman went to bed that night with an uneasy feeling. When he did fall asleep, he slept very soundly, for he had walked a long way that day. His wife, the new queen, however, could not get to sleep. She turned from side to side all night wondering what else she could ask for. At the break of day she saw the sun come up. "Ha!" she thought, "could I not order the sun and the moon to appear when I want them to?"

"Husband," she said, and hit him in the side with her arm, "wake up; go to the fish and tell him I want to control the sun and moon."

The man was still half asleep but he was so afraid that he fell out of bed. "What did you say, wife?"

"Husband, if I can't order the sun and moon to come up then I don't see the point in having everything else. Go now, to the fish, I want to be master of the sun and moon."

"Oh no!" said the man falling to his knees, "the fish can't do that. He has made you queen, be happy with that."

■uneasy 形不安な　■side to side 左右に　■break of day 夜明け　■fall to one's knee 崩れ落ちて膝をつく

漁師とおかみさん

　おかみさんは亭主をしばらく見つめたが、何も言わなかった。その夜、漁師は落ち着かない気分で床についた。けれども、いったん寝入ると、ぐっすりとよく眠った。その日は一日じゅうかけずり回っていたからだ。ところが、新しい女王になったおかみさんは、寝つくことができなかった。一晩じゅう寝返りを打って、ほかに何になれるか考えた。夜明けになり、おかみさんは日が昇るのを見た。「そうだ！」おかみさんは考えた。「日や月を、自分の好きな時間に昇らすことはできないものかしら？」

　「ねえ、あんた」と、おかみさんは言うと、亭主の横腹をつついた。「起きてよ。魚のところに行って、あたしが日や月を思うように動かしたいと言っていると伝えとくれ」

　亭主はまだ半分眠っていたが、あんまり驚いたものだから、ベッドから転がり落ちた。「何て言ったんだ、おまえ？」

　「あんた、日や月を思い通りに昇らせられなければ、何もかも手に入れたって意味がないんだよ。さあ、魚のところに行っとくれ。あたしは日と月の主人になりたいんだ」

　「何てことを！」亭主は両膝をついた。「魚にはそんなことできやしない。おまえを女王にしてくれたのだから、それで十分と思え」

The Fisherman and His Wife

His wife looked at him and became almost mad with anger. She tore at her clothes then gave her husband a mighty push, "Go to the fish this minute. I can't stand this any longer." The man ran off afraid of going to the sea, but more afraid of his wife. Outside there was a storm, the like of which the man had never seen before. The wind blew cold rain into his face as he stood facing the sea. The waves were as high as mountains and the water looked black with anger. In his fear he cried out:

"Great fish in the sea, please listen to me,
 My wife won't let be, as I'd have it be."

"What does she want?" asked the fish.
"My wife wants to be master of the sun and moon."
"Go home," said the fish, "she is back in your old house already."

And there they have remained to this day.

■tore 動tear（引き裂く）の過去　■this minute 今すぐ　■run off 逃げ去る　■face 動 ～の方を向く　■in one's fear おどおどして

漁師とおかみさん

　おかみさんは亭主を見つめ、怒りで気が狂いそうになった。それから、自分の服を引き裂き、亭主を力一杯、押した。「すぐに、魚のところに行くんだよ。もう、これ以上、こんなことに耐えられない」。亭主は急いで逃げ出した。海に行くのは怖かったが、それ以上におかみさんが怖かった。外は、見たこともないような嵐だった。亭主が海に向かって立つと、風が冷たい雨を顔に打ちつけた。波は山のように高く、水は怒りでまっ黒に見えた。おどおどと、亭主は大声で叫んだ。

「海の大きな魚さん、どうか聞いとくれ。
　わしがいいと言っても、女房が言うことを聞かないんだ」

「おかみさんは何がほしいと言うのだね？」魚がたずねた。
「女房は、日と月の主人になりたいと言うんだ」
「家にお帰り」魚が言った。「おかみさんはもう元の古い家に戻っているよ」
　そういうわけで、今日までずっと、夫婦はそこに暮らしている。

覚えておきたい英語表現

> Not a bad price *for* three nights' work.（p. 98, 5行目)
> 三泊の仕事にしては悪くない値段だよ。

　forは「〜のために」という意味で使われることが多い印象がありますがとても多義で用法の多い単語です。この表現で使われているforは「〜の割には」という意味で、基準を超えた意外さを表します。

　3日間にわたって夜働けば、お姫様の一人と結婚できて将来は王になることができる可能性があるので、兵士は「割が良い仕事」と言っているのです。確かに誰が考えても割がいい仕事ですね…失敗したら文字通り首が飛ぶのですが！

　「〜の割には」の意味を持つforの用法はとても便利です。ぜひ覚えましょう。

【例文】

　　He looks young *for* his age.
　　彼は年齢の割には若く見える。

　　It's cold *for* June.
　　6月にしては寒い。

　　Tom plays the piano well *for* a beginner.
　　トムは初心者にしては上手にピアノを演奏する。

　ちなみにNot a bad 〜という表現にも注目してください。ネイティブスピーカーはNot bad. という表現をよく使います。

　　A: Tastes good?　　美味しい？
　　B: *Not bad.*

といった感じです。badは「悪い」ですからNot bad. は「悪くないね」という直訳になります。日本語で「悪くないね」と聞くと、「良いならGoodと言うだろう。悪くはないけど良くもない、まあまあって感じかな？」という印象を持つ方が多いのではないでしょうか。

Not badを英英辞典で引くと "fairly good" と書いてあります。つまり「かなり良い」です。Not so bad. も同様です。つまり Not bad. は結構「褒めレベル」が高い言葉なのです。英語を日本語で理解するのではなく、英語を英語で理解する習慣を身に付けたいものです。

　さらに言えば、表現の意味を理解したら、さらに一歩進んで「状況に応じた使い方」まで習得することを心掛けましょう。「知っている」レベルから、「適切な状況で使える」レベルに英語力を向上させなければ、知っている英語表現を使いこなすことはできません。

How could this poor soldier *do any better*? (p. 100, 19行目)
この哀れな兵士に何ができるっていうの？

　眠ったふりをしている兵士を見て、年長の姫が言ったセリフです。How could (can) Ｓ Ｖ ? で「どうすればＳはＶできるの？」「よくもＳがＶできるもんだ」といった話し手の驚きや呆れた気持ちを表します。疑問文の形をしていますが相手の答えを期待しているわけではありません。

　　How could you do so stupid?
　　一体なんでそんな馬鹿げたことができたの？

　　How can you say so?
　　よくもそんなことが言えたね。
　　＊省略してHow can you?の形もあり「ひどい、信じられない、よくもまあ」といった気持ちを表します。

　any は「何か」better は good の比較級で「より良い」を意味します。今までチャレンジした王子たちがうまくいかなかったことと比べて、「今までの王子以上の良い結果を出せるとは思えない」という意味がこめられているために "do any better" が用いられています。

Part 4

The Brave Little Tailor
勇ましいちびの仕立て屋

The Golden Goose
金のガチョウ

The Brave Little Tailor

One fine summer morning a little tailor sat at his table by the window working as fast as he could. As he was working, a country woman came down the road outside his house calling, "Lovely sweets, get your lovely sweets here." The little tailor loved sweets so he called out of the window, "Come up here my dear woman, for here is a market for your goods."

　The woman climbed the stairs with her heavy bag and unpacked all her sweets. After smelling all of them the tailor chose one. It was a sticky, sugary sweet that he was sure he would enjoy. "I'll take half a small bag of this one," he said, at last.

■tailor 名仕立て屋　■lovely 形おいしい　■market 名需要
■unpack 動荷を解く　■sticky 形ねばねばする

勇ましいちびの仕立て屋

　あるお天気のいい夏の朝、ちびの仕立て屋が窓のそばにあるテーブルの前に座り、せっせと働いていた。そうしていると、田舎から来た物売りの女が家の外の通りを歩いて来て呼びかけた。「おいしいジャムだよ。甘いジャムがあるよ」。ちびの仕立て屋はジャムが好きなので、窓から呼びかけた。「こっちに上がって来てくれないか、おばさん。あんたの品物をほしがっている者がいるよ」

　物売りの女は、重いカバンを持って階段を上がり、品物を全部広げた。仕立て屋はそれぞれのにおいを嗅いでから、ひとつ選んだ。それは、ねばねばした甘いジャムで、とてもおいしそうだった。そして、とうとう「これを小さな袋半分もらうよ」と言った。

The Brave Little Tailor

The woman, who had hoped to sell a lot more than that, gave him the small bag and went on her way looking rather unkindly at the tailor. "I shall not eat these sweets right away," cried the tailor, "No, I will save them until I have finished work." So he laid the sweets on a table by the wall and went back to the clothes he was making.

The smell of the sweets, however, caused many flies to come to the tailor's room. They landed on the sweets and began tasting them.

"Who said you could have some?" said the little tailor as he attempted to drive them away. But the flies did not understand his language and they came back for more in greater numbers. Then the little tailor became really angry and hit at the flies with a cloth. He got seven, all dead with their legs in the air, at one stroke.

"What a man I am," he said, "the whole town should hear of what I have done." As fast as he could, he cut himself a belt, and on it he wrote the words, "Seven at one stroke!" Proudly, he put it on and looked at himself.

■unkindly 副 意地悪に　■fly 名 ハエ　■attempt to ～しようと試みる　■drive ～ away ～を追い払う　■stroke 名 一打

勇ましいちびの仕立て屋

　物売りの女は、もっとたくさん売れると思っていたので、小さな袋をわたすと、仕立て屋をちょっと意地悪そうに見て、帰っていった。「すぐに食べないでおこう」仕立て屋が叫んだ。「そうだ、仕事が終わるまで取っておくんだ」。それで、ジャムを壁のそばにあるテーブルの上に置き、作りかけの服に取りかかった。

　ところが、ジャムのにおいに誘われて、たくさんのハエが部屋に入って来た。ハエはジャムの上にたかり、食べはじめた。

　「だれが食べていいと言った？」ちびの仕立て屋はハエを追い払おうとした。ところがハエには仕立て屋の言葉がわからず、ますます大勢集まって戻って来た。すると、仕立て屋は本気で怒り出し、布でハエをたたいた。たった一打ちで7匹つかまえると、どれも足を上に向けて死んでいた。

　「ぼくは何と勇ましい男だろう」仕立て屋が言った。「ぼくのしたことを、町じゅうに知らせなくてはな」。仕立て屋は大急ぎで帯を裁ち、その上に「一打ちで7つ！」と書いた。得意そうに、それを身に着け自分の姿を見つめた。

The Brave Little Tailor

"No, not the whole town, but the whole world should know of me." The tailor looked around his room realizing that it had become too small for someone as mighty as he. He decided to leave. The only thing he took with him was a small piece of cheese, which he put in his pocket.

He decided to journey throughout the world until he was famous everywhere. As he rushed outside he saw a bird caught in a hedge. Feeling sorry for it he gently picked it out and put it in his pocket with the cheese.

He stepped out happily, and being small and light he could walk a long way without feeling tired. The road led to a mountain, but the tailor just kept going up and up. When he reached the highest point he found a powerful giant sitting there. The tailor was not afraid and he went up to the giant and said, "Good day, friend. Are you sitting here looking at the great world beyond? I am on my way there, do you want to come with me?"

The giant looked down upon the tailor, "You," he said in a deep, loud voice, "who are you to offer yourself as a traveling companion for a giant? You are a weak nobody."

■mighty 形強大な ■journey 動旅に出る ■hedge 名生垣 ■companion 名仲間
■weak 形弱い ■nobody 名取るに足らない人

勇ましいちびの仕立て屋

「いや、町じゅうではだめだ。世界じゅうにぼくのことを知らせなくては」。仕立て屋は部屋を見回し、自分のような勇ましい者にはこの部屋は狭くなったと感じた。それで、そこを出ることにした。部屋から小さな一かけらのチーズだけを持ち出し、それをポケットに入れた。

仕立て屋は世界じゅうを旅して、あちこちで有名になるんだと決心した。急いで外に出ると、小鳥がやぶにからまっていた。かわいそうに思って、やさしく小鳥をつかむと、チーズといっしょにポケットに入れた。

仕立て屋はうれしそうに歩き出した。体が小さくて軽いので、長い距離を疲れないで歩くことができた。道は山に通じていたが、どんどん登っていった。頂上に着くと、そこには力持ちの巨人が座っていた。仕立て屋は恐れることもなく巨人に近づいて話しかけた。「こんにちは、兄弟分。そこに座って、向こうのすばらしい世界を見ているのかい？ ぼくはそこに行く途中なんだ。いっしょに来ないかい？」

巨人は仕立て屋をさげすむように見て、「おい」と、低くて大きな声で言った。「巨人を旅の道連れにしようというおまえは何者だ？ 弱くて取るに足らない奴のくせに」

The Brave Little Tailor

"You think so, do you?" replied the tailor, "well, just you look at this." He opened his coat and showed the giant his belt. "Read there what sort of man I am."

The giant read, "Seven at one stroke." He of course thought that it was seven men that the tailor had killed at one stroke and decided that he should be a little careful with the small, strange fellow. "I know," thought the giant, "I'll find out how strong he is." He picked up a stone and crushed it in his large hands until water came out of it.

"If you really have any strength you will be able to do the same."

"That is child's play for someone like me," replied the little tailor. He took the cheese out of his pocket and crushed it until it was wet through.

The giant did not know what to say but he was still doubtful of the little man's power, so he picked up another stone and threw it so high that it almost went out of sight.

"Now," he said, "you do that!"

■fellow 图やつ、男　■crush 動押しつぶす　■child's play 朝飯前のこと　■wet through びしょびしょになる　■doubtful 形本当とは思えない

勇ましいちびの仕立て屋

「そう思うかい？」仕立て屋が答えた。「それじゃ、ちょっとこれを見てくれ」。そう言うと、上着の前をあけて、巨人に帯を見せた。「さあ、読んでみろ。ぼくがどんな男かわかるよ」

巨人が読むと、「一打ちで7つ」と書いてあった。もちろん、仕立て屋が一打ちで殺したのは7人の人間だと思い、このちびで奇妙な奴に少し用心することにした。「いい考えがあるぞ」と巨人は考えた。「こいつがどれだけ強いか試してやろう」。巨人が石を拾い、大きな両手で握りつぶすと、水がたらたらとこぼれた。

「おまえが本当に強いのなら、同じことができるはずだ」

「そんなこと、ぼくにとっては子どもの遊びさ」ちびの仕立て屋が答え、ポケットからチーズを取り出して握りつぶすと、汁が流れ出た。

巨人は言葉を失ったが、ちびの男の力をまだ信じることができなかった。それで、別の石を拾って投げ上げると、石は高く上がり、ほとんど見えなくなった。

「さあ」巨人が言った。「おまえの番だ！」

The Brave Little Tailor

"Well thrown, I'll give you that," replied the tailor, "but your stone fell to earth again. I will throw one that won't come down again."

He took the bird from his pocket and threw it into the air. The bird, happy to be free, was quick to fly high into the sky and was soon out of sight. "There what do you think of that, my friend?" asked the tailor.

"Well, I agree that you can throw, but now I'll see if you can carry a heavy weight," answered the giant.

He led the little tailor to a mighty tree that had fallen and lay on the ground. "If you are strong enough, help me carry this out of the wood."

"With pleasure," said the little man. "You take the trunk on your shoulder, and I will carry the branches, which is the most difficult part."

The giant took the trunk on his shoulders, and the tailor seated himself on a branch. As the giant could not look around, he had to carry not only the whole tree, but the tailor as well.

■I'll give you that それについては（言い分などを）認めよう　■see if ～かどうか確かめる　■with pleasure 喜んで　■trunk 名幹

勇ましいちびの仕立て屋

「よく投げたね。その点は認めるよ」仕立て屋が答えた。「だけど、あんたの石はまた地面に落ちただろ。ぼくは決して地面に落ちないように投げてみせるよ」

仕立て屋はポケットから小鳥を取り出し、空に向かって投げた。小鳥は自由になって喜び、急いで空高く舞い上がり、すぐに見えなくなった。「さあ、これでどうだい、兄弟分?」仕立て屋が訊いた。

「なるほど、投げるのは確かにうまい。だが、今度はおまえが重い物を運べるか確かめてやる」巨人が答えた。

巨人は仕立て屋を、倒れて地面に転がっている大木のところに連れていった。「おまえが力持ちなら、この木を森から運び出すのを手伝え」

「いいとも」小さな男が答えた。「あんたは幹を肩にかつぎ、ぼくは枝を持つよ。ここが一番重いんだぞ」

巨人が幹を肩にかつぐと、仕立て屋は枝の上に座った。巨人は振り返ることができなかったので、木をまるごと1本と、おまけに仕立て屋も運ぶはめになった。

The Brave Little Tailor

The little man was really enjoying himself and even started singing one of his favorite songs, as if carrying a tree was the easiest thing in the world.

The giant, after he had carried the heavy tree some distance, was out of breath and called out that he must stop and rest.

The tailor jumped off, caught hold of the tree with both arms as if he had been carrying it all the way and said to the giant, "To think that a big fellow like you can't even carry a tree!"

They walked on together until they came to a fruit tree. The giant quickly took hold of the top of the tree, where the sweetest fruit grew and pulled it towards the ground. He told the tailor to eat as much fruit as he wanted and put the tree in the little man's hands. When the giant let go, the tailor was too weak to hold it, and the tree, springing back into the air, carried the tailor with it.

When he jumped unhurt to the ground, the giant cried, "Didn't you have enough strength to hold that small tree?"

■out of breath 息を切らして　■catch hold of 〜をつかむ　■take hold of 〜をつかむ
■spring back 跳ね返る　■unhurt 形 無傷の

勇ましいちびの仕立て屋

　小さな男は陽気にはしゃぎ、お気に入りの歌を1曲、歌いさえした。まるで、木を運ぶことはこの世で一番楽なことだといわんばかりだった。

　巨人は重い木を少し遠くまで運ぶと息が切れたので、止まって休みたいと大声で言った。

　仕立て屋は枝から跳び下り、両腕で木をかかえ、まるでずっと運んでいたように見せて、巨人に言った。「あんたのような大男が1本の木さえ運べないとはな！」

　2人はいっしょに歩いていき、1本の果物の木のところまで来た。巨人はすぐに木のてっぺんをつかんだ。そこには一番熟した果物がなっていて、巨人はそれを地面に引き寄せた。そして、好きなだけ食べろと言って、木を小さな男の両手に持たせた。巨人が手を離すと、仕立て屋にはそれを押さえているだけの力がなかったので、木は仕立て屋もろとも、空中に跳ね上がった。

　仕立て屋が怪我もなく地面に跳び下りると、巨人が叫んだ。「こんな小さな木さえ押さえる力もないのか？」

The Brave Little Tailor

"It has nothing to do with strength, my dear fellow, do you suppose that I, who have killed seven at one stroke, could not have done it? I jumped over the tree simply because I saw a hunter about to take a shot at me. Jump it yourself, if you can."

The giant made an attempt but could not clear the tree and found himself caught up in the branches, so once again the little tailor got the best of him.

When he had got down the giant said, "As you are such a brave fellow, come and stay with us tonight."

The tailor followed the giant to his home where he saw many other giants. They were sitting around a fire eating large amounts of food, and they looked at the tailor as though they would eat him too. Then the giant showed him a bed and told him to lie down and rest. The bed was too big for the tailor so he went over to one side and slept in a corner.

In the middle of the night, when the giant thought that the tailor was asleep, he took an iron nail and drove it into the middle of the bed, and thought he had made an end of the objectionable little man.

■about to まさに〜しようとしている　■make an attempt 試みる　■catch up 〜を絡ませる　■iron nail 鉄釘　■objectionable 形不愉快な

勇ましいちびの仕立て屋

「力とは関係ないよ、兄弟分。一打ちで7つもやっつけたこのぼくが、そんなことをできないとでも考えているのかね？ 木を跳び越したのは、ただ、猟師がぼくを撃とうとしたのが見えたからさ。あんたも跳んでみろよ。やれるものならね」

巨人はやってみたが、木を跳び越すことができず、枝に引っかかってしまった。というわけで、またもやちびの仕立て屋の勝ちだった。

巨人は木から降りると、言った。「おまえはとても勇ましい奴だから、今夜はおれたちのところに来て泊れよ」

仕立て屋が巨人のあとについて住みかに行くと、ほかにもたくさんの巨人がいた。火を囲んで座り、たらふく食べ物を食べていた。そうしながらも、おまえも食べてしまうぞというような目で、仕立て屋をにらみつけた。そのあとで、巨人は仕立て屋にベッドをあてがい、横になって休んでくれと言った。ベッドは大きすぎたので、仕立て屋は片側に行き、隅っこで寝た。

真夜中になり、巨人は仕立て屋が眠っていると思い、鉄の釘をベッドのまんなかに打ち込み、これで不愉快な小さな男を始末できたと考えた。

The Brave Little Tailor

At break of day, the giants went out into the woods thinking that the tailor was dead. A little later, however, the tailor came walking towards them as lively and happy as ever. The giants then became very afraid, and they thought the tailor would kill them so they ran away as fast as they could. The tailor, who knew nothing of the attempt on his life, thought that this was rather strange of the giants, but decided to continue on his journey to see the world.

After walking for some time he came to a large palace and he decided to rest before entering. As he lay sleeping on the ground, people came out of the palace to look at him. They read what was written on his belt, "Seven at one stroke!"

"Ah!" they thought, "this must be a great soldier." Some of them went to the king and told him of the "great soldier," saying that if a war broke out he would be a very useful man to have around.

■as ~ as ever 相変わらず~で ■lively 形元気いっぱいの ■know nothing of ~について一切知らない ■break out 勃発する

勇ましいちびの仕立て屋

　夜明けになり、巨人たちは森に出ていき、仕立て屋は死んだものと思っていた。ところが少したつと、死んだはずの男が歩いて近づいて来て、おまけに相変わらず元気でうれしそうにしている。巨人たちはとても怖くなり、仕立て屋に殺されると思い込んで、一目散に逃げ出した。仕立て屋は、命を狙われたことなど知らないので、巨人はかなり奇妙な行動をするものだと思ったが、そのまま旅を続けて世界を見にいくことにした。

　しばらく歩くと大きな宮殿に着いたので、なかに入る前に休むことにした。地面の上で横になって眠っていると、宮殿から人々が出てきて、仕立て屋を眺めた。人々は、帯に「一打ちで7つ！」と書かれているのを読んだ。

　「おやおや」人々は考えた。「この人は偉大な兵隊にちがいない」。何人かが王様のところに行き、「偉大な兵隊」の話をし、戦争がはじまったら、そばに置いておくととても役に立つでしょうと進言した。

The Brave Little Tailor

The king thought this was a good idea and sent one of his men to offer the "great soldier" a position in the army. The man watched over the sleeping tailor and, when he opened his eyes, made the offer.

"This was the reason I came here," answered the tailor. "I am ready to enter the king's service."

He was received with great honor and given a special house to live in. The other soldiers in the king's army, however, did not like the tailor. They were afraid that if he got angry with them he could kill seven of them with each stroke. So they all went to the king together and resigned because of the tailor.

The king was sorry to lose all his soldiers because of one man. But he too was afraid of the tailor and did not want to tell him to go. So he tried to think of a plan to remove the tailor from his kingdom without making him angry. He thought for a long time; then at last he hit on a plan. He sent for the little tailor and told him a story.

■position 名地位 ■service 名軍隊 ■resign 動辞任する ■hit on ふと思いつく

勇ましいちびの仕立て屋

　王様は、それはいい考えだと思い、家来のひとりをやり、「偉大な兵隊」に軍隊の重要な地位を申し出させることにした。家来は眠っている仕立て屋を見つめていたが、仕立て屋が目を覚ますと、言われた通り、申し出を伝えた。

　「ぼくは、そのためにやって来たんです」仕立て屋が答えた。「王様の軍隊に入る用意はできています」。

　仕立て屋はうやうやしく迎えられ、特別な住まいを与えられた。ところが、王様の軍隊のほかの軍人たちは、仕立て屋を気に入らなかった。怒らせたら、一打ちごとに7人も殺してしまうことを恐れたのだ。それで、軍人たちはみないっしょに王様のところに行き、仕立て屋のせいで軍隊をやめると申し出た。

　王様はひとりの男のために、自分の軍人をみんな失ったことを残念がった。ところが、王様も仕立て屋を恐れていたので、出て行けとは言えなかった。それで、仕立て屋を怒らせずに、自分の王国から追い出す計画を立てようとした。長いあいだ考えていたが、とうとう、よい計画を思いついた。王様は仕立て屋を呼びにやり、こんな話を聞かせた。

The Brave Little Tailor

In a certain wood in his kingdom lived two giants. Everyone was afraid of them because they took money off of anybody they met and killed anyone who tried to stand up to them. The king told the tailor that if he overcame and killed the giants he would give him the hand of his only daughter in marriage and half his kingdom.

The little tailor did not take too long to think about it.

"Of course I will do it. It is not every day that you get offered a beautiful princess and half a kingdom. A man who can kill seven at a stroke is more than a match for two."

The next day the tailor set off. When he reached the wood, he started looking for the giants. After a while, he saw them sleeping under a tree. The little tailor quickly filled his pockets with stones and went up the tree. When he was on the branch immediately above the giants, he started to drop stones on one of them. For a long time the giant did not move but when he did wake up he pushed his companion and asked, "Why are you hitting me?"

■take ~ off ～を取り上げる　■stand up to ～にはむかう　■overcome 動 ～に打ち勝つ　■hand 名 婚約、誓約　■take too long 時間がかかり過ぎる　■match for ～に匹敵する

勇ましいちびの仕立て屋

　「王国の森に、2人の巨人が住んでいる。だれもが巨人を恐れているが、それは、巨人がだれかれかまわずに、会った者からお金を巻き上げ、はむかう者はだれでも殺してしまうからだ」。そのあとで、王様は仕立て屋に言った。「おまえが巨人をやっつけて殺してくれたなら、ひとり娘との結婚を認め、王国の半分を与える」

　ちびの仕立て屋は考え込んだりしなかった。
　「もちろん、そうします。美しい姫と王国の半分をいただけることなんて、毎日あることではありませんからね。一打ちで7つの男なら、2人の巨人など相手ではありません」

　次の日、仕立て屋は出発した。森に着くと、巨人を捜しはじめた。しばらくすると、2人の巨人が木の下で寝ているのを見つけた。ちびの仕立て屋は急いでポケットに石を一杯詰めて、その木に登った。巨人たちの真上の枝まで来ると、巨人のひとりに石を落としはじめた。長いあいだ巨人は動かなかったが、目を覚ますと仲間をつついてたずねた。「どうしておれを殴るのだ？」

The Brave Little Tailor

"You're dreaming," replied the other giant, "I didn't hit you."

Again they lay down to sleep, and again the little tailor dropped a stone, this time on the second giant.

"What's that?" cried the giant, "Why are you hitting me?"

"I am not hitting you," answered the first giant in an angry voice, "now stop waking me up." After a few angry words they settled down to try to sleep. The little tailor renewed his game, picked his biggest stone and dropped it on the head of the first giant.

"This is too much," shouted the giant and he jumped up like a madman. He picked up his companion and pushed him back against the tree with such force that the tailor had to hold on with both hands to stop himself from falling out. With one powerful blow the second giant knocked the first one to the floor and then a mighty fight took place. The giants pulled up trees and hit each other over the head until at last they both lay dead on the ground.

■settle down 落ち着く ■renew 動〜を再び始める ■madman 名狂人 ■knock 〜 to the floor 〜を地面に打ちのめす ■take place（事件などが）起こる

勇ましいちびの仕立て屋

「寝ぼけているのだな」もうひとりの巨人が答えた。「おまえを殴ったりしないぞ」

ふたたび、巨人たちは横になって眠り、またもや仕立て屋は石を落したが、今回は2番目の巨人に落とした。

「何だこれは？」2番目の巨人が叫んだ。「どうしておれを殴るんだ？」

「おまえを殴ってなんかいないぞ」最初の巨人が怒って言った。「もう、おれを起こさないでくれ」。2人はしばらく言い争っていたが、気を落ち着かせてまた眠ろうとした。ちびの仕立て屋はもう一度いたずらをはじめ、一番大きい石をつかむと最初の巨人の頭に落とした。

「もうたくさんだ」最初の巨人は叫び、気が狂ったように跳び上がった。仲間をつかみ上げ、ものすごい力で木に押しつけたので、仕立て屋は両手で木にしっかりつかまり、落ちないようにしなければならなかった。2番目の巨人が力強い一撃で相手を地面に打ちのめすと、激しい戦いがはじまった。巨人たちは木を引き抜くと、互いに頭に打ちつけ、とうとう2人とも地面にのびて死んでしまった。

The Brave Little Tailor

The tailor quickly jumped down from his tree, drew his sword and pushed it into the body of each of the giants. He then called out to the servants who had accompanied him as far as the wood, to come and see what he had done. The servants could hardly believe their eyes; there were fallen trees everywhere and, lying side by side in their own blood, were the two giants.

When he returned to the palace he demanded that the king fulfill his promise. But the king tried to think of a way to put him off.

"Before you win my daughter and half of my kingdom I require you to do another great act. You must catch a dangerous unicorn that is wild in the wood."

"I am even less afraid of unicorns than I am of giants," said the tailor.

Once again he entered the wood leaving his servants outside. He quickly saw the unicorn, which made straight for him. He stood quite still, and, when the unicorn charged him, he jumped quickly behind a tree. The unicorn could not stop and hit the tree so hard that its horn got stuck in it.

■drew 動draw（引く）の過去　■accompany 動同伴する　■side by side 並んで
■put ~ off ~をはぐらかす　■win 動 ~を獲得する　■stand still じっと立っている
■charge 動突進する　■horn 名角　■stuck in ~にはまり込む

勇ましいちびの仕立て屋

　仕立て屋は素早く木から跳び下り、剣を抜き、それぞれの巨人の体を突き刺した。そのあとで森のはずれまでお供した家来たちに、こっちに来て自分のしたことを見ろと大きな声で叫んだ。家来たちは自分の目を疑った。あちこちに木が倒れ、2人の巨人が血まみれになって、並んで横たわっていたのだ。

　仕立て屋は宮殿に戻ると、王様に約束を守ってほしいと要求した。ところが王様は約束を延ばす方法を考えていた。

「おまえに娘と王国の半分をやる前に、もうひとつ大きな仕事をしてもらう。森で暴れている危険な一角獣をつかまえて来るんだ」

「わたしは巨人だって怖くないのに、まして一角獣なんか怖いわけがありません」仕立て屋が答えた。

　ふたたび、仕立て屋は森に入ったが、家来たちを外で待たせた。一角獣はすぐに見つかり、仕立て屋めがけて突進してきた。小さな男は動かずにじっと立ち、一角獣が襲ってくると、素早く木のうしろに跳び込んだ。一角獣は止まることができず、激しく木にぶつかったので、角が木に突き刺さった。

The Brave Little Tailor

"Now I have you," said the tailor and he cut off the unicorn's horn with his sword. Without its sharp horn the unicorn was no longer dangerous, and the tailor was able to lead the animal peacefully back to the king.

But the king still did not keep his promise. "Before we set a date for the wedding you must catch one last wild animal still free in the wood. It's a danger to everyone."

"I will go with pleasure," said the tailor; "hunting this animal will be child's play for me."

When the animal saw the tailor it rushed at him angrily ready to knock him over. The tailor was too quick for him, however, and ran into an old house that was nearby. When the animal rushed in after him, the tailor jumped out of the window, ran round the house and closed the door. The angry animal tried to get through the window but was far too heavy and ended up lying unhappily on the floor.

■rush at 〜に突進する　■knock 〜 over 〜を張り倒す　■rush in 〜に突入する
■get through 〜を通り抜ける　■end up 〜する羽目になる

勇ましいちびの仕立て屋

「さあ、つかまえたぞ」と仕立て屋は言って、剣で角を切り取った。とがった角がなければ、一角獣はまったく危険ではなかった。それで、仕立て屋は野獣を無事に王様の前に連れていくことができた。

ところが、王様はまた約束を守らなかった。「婚礼の日取りを決める前に、まだ森をうろついている最後のけものをつかまえるのだ。だれにとっても危険だからな」

「喜んで参ります」仕立て屋が言った。「そのようなけものをつかまえることなど、わたしにとっては子供の遊びです」

けものは仕立て屋を見ると、怒って突進し、まさに引き倒そうとした。ところが仕立て屋は思わぬ速さで、近くの古い小屋に逃げ込んだ。けものが追いかけて小屋に突入してくると、仕立て屋は窓から跳び出し、小屋のまわりを走って、戸を閉めた。怒ったけものは窓から跳び出そうとしたが、重すぎて出られず、情けないことに、最後には床に転がった。

The Brave Little Tailor

After his latest success the tailor returned to the king and demanded that he honor his promise. The king had no choice and the wedding went ahead although both he and his daughter, the princess, were unhappy. The tailor was, of course, very happy; he was now a king with a beautiful wife.

Soon afterwards the new queen heard her husband talking in his sleep one night. He was talking about his old job and speaking about the clothes he had made. She then realized what her husband had been before he came to her father's kingdom. Not a "great soldier," but a simple tailor! The next morning she went to her father and told him that he had married her off to a poor tailor.

The old king thought about it for a moment then replied, "Tonight leave your bedroom door open; when he is asleep my soldiers will come in, tie him up and put him on a ship that will take him to the other side of the world."

However, the tailor's servant, and only real friend, had heard this plan and told his master what the old king wanted to do.

■honor one's promise 約束を守る　■latest 形 最後の　■go ahead 進行する
■simple 形 たんなる　■marry ~ off ~を嫁がせる

勇ましいちびの仕立て屋

　けものを仕留めると、仕立て屋は王様のところに行き、約束を守るように迫った。王様は、もはやどうすることもできなかったので、とうとう結婚式が行われた。けれども王様も娘の姫も、少しもうれしくなかった。仕立て屋と言えば、王様になり、美しい妻をもらったのだから、もちろん、とても喜んだ。

　それからしばらくしたある晩のこと、新しいお后は、夫が寝言を言うのを聞いた。夫は昔の仕事のことを話し、自分の作った服のことをしゃべった。そういうわけでお后は、夫が父親の王国に来る前に何をしていたのか知った。「偉大な兵隊」なんかではなく、ただの仕立て屋だったのだ！次の朝、お后は父親のところに行き、王様が自分を貧しい仕立て屋と結婚させたと訴えた。

　年寄りの王様は、しばらく考えて答えた。「今夜はおまえの寝室の戸をあけておきなさい。あの男が寝入ったら、わしの兵隊が踏み込んで縛り上げ、船にのせる。船はあの男を世界の向こう側まで運んでくれるだろう」

　ところが、仕立て屋の家来で、ただひとりの信頼できる友人が、このたくらみを聞きつけ、年寄りの王様が何を望んでいるか、主人に伝えた。

The Brave Little Tailor

"Don't worry," said the tailor, "I'll stop their little plan."

That night he went to bed at the same time as usual and lay down by his wife. When his wife thought he was asleep, she got up and opened the door. Almost at once the tailor started talking, but this time he was not really asleep. "I have killed seven at one stroke, killed two giants, caught a unicorn and a wild animal; is it likely that I would be afraid of someone waiting outside my bedroom?"

When the soldiers heard the tailor talking like this, they became very fearful, and instead of tying him up they ran away. From then on nobody ever dared to lay a finger on him. The brave little tailor remained king to the end of his days.

■little 形 取るに足らない　■at once 即座に　■dare to 大胆にも~する　■lay a finger on ~に手をかける

勇ましいちびの仕立て屋

「心配することはない」仕立て屋が言った。「そんなくだらないたくらみなんか止めてみせる」

その夜、仕立て屋はいつもと同じ時刻に床につき、妻のそばに横たわった。妻は夫が眠ったと判断すると、起き上がって戸をあけた。それとほぼ同時に、仕立て屋が話しはじめた。ただし、今回は本当に眠っていたのではなかった。「わたしは一打ちで7つやっつけ、2人の巨人を殺し、一角獣と荒々しいけものをつかまえた。だれかが寝室の外で待ちかまえているからって、わたしが恐れるとでも思うか？」

兵隊たちは仕立て屋がそのようなことを口走るのを聞くと、ひどく怯え出し、その小さな男を縛り上げるどころか、逃げ出した。それ以後、その男に手をかけようなどとするものは、だれもいなくなった。勇ましいちびの仕立て屋は、死ぬまで王様をつとめた。

The Golden Goose

Once there was a man who had three sons. The youngest, called Dunderhead, was thought to be a fool by the other two sons. They were always telling him how foolish he was and generally made his life unpleasant.

One day the eldest brother wanted to go into the forest to cut some wood. Before he left, his mother gave him a freshly cooked cake and a bottle of wine to take for his dinner. On the edge of the forest he met a gray-haired old man, who wished him good day and asked for a piece of the cake and some wine, as he had not had food or drink for some time.

■once 副かつて　■dunderhead 名まぬけ《古》　■unpleasant 形不愉快な　■edge 名端

金のガチョウ

　むかしむかし、ひとりの男がいて、その人には3人の息子がいた。末の息子は「ぬけ作」と呼ばれ、2人の兄にばかにされていた。いつも兄たちに愚か者だとあざけられて、弟はたいてい、いやな思いをして過ごしていた。

　ある日、長男が森に行って、木を切りたいと思った。出かける前に、母親が焼きたてのパンケーキとワイン1瓶を昼ごはんに持たせた。森のはずれで、長男は白髪頭の老人に出会った。老人は長男にこんにちはと言って、パンケーキ一切れとワインを少しわけてほしいと頼んだ。しばらくのあいだ、何も飲んだり食べたりしていなかったからだ。

The Golden Goose

The son answered, "Why should I give you my cake and wine? I would have less myself. Be off with you."

He continued into the forest leaving the gray-haired old man behind him. He started cutting wood but soon made a bad stroke and hit his arm, and he was forced to return home to rest.

The second son then went into the forest and his mother gave him some cake and wine. He too passed the old man, who asked for some food. "Get your own food, old man," replied the second son, "Why should I give you mine?" He then started to cut wood but before long had hit his own leg and had to be carried home.

Then Dunderhead asked his father if he could go and cut wood.

"Look what happened to the other two when they went. You, who have no sense, had better not go to the forest."

But Dunderhead kept asking his father until at last he was allowed to go. Instead of cake and wine his mother gave him some dry bread and water. As he was entering the forest, the gray-haired old man came up to him and asked him for food and something to drink.

■be off with you あっちへ行け ■stroke 図打つこと ■keep doing 〜し続ける
■until at last ついに〜するまで ■come up to 〜までやって来る

金のガチョウ

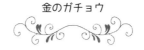

　長男が答えた。「何でおれのパンケーキとワインをあげなきゃならないんだ？　おれの取り分が減るじゃないか。あっちへ行ってくれ」
　長男は森のなかに入ってゆき、白髪頭の老人を置き去りにした。木を切りはじめたが、すぐに打ちそこなって、自分の腕を打った。それで家に戻り休まなくてはならなくなった。

　その後、次男が森に行くときも、母親はパンケーキとワインを持たせた。次男も白髪頭の老人の前を通り、食べ物をわけてほしいと頼まれた。「自分の食べ物くらい何とかしろよ、じいさん」次男が答えた。「何でおれの物をあげなきゃならないんだ？」。そう言うと、次男は木を切りはじめたが、すぐに自分の脚を切ってしまい、家に運ばれることになった。

　その後、ぬけ作が父親に自分も森に行って木を切りたいと頼んだ。

「兄さんたちが出かけてどうなったか見てごらん。おまえは何もわかっちゃいないんだから、森に行かないほうがいい」
　けれども、ぬけ作は父親に頼み続けたので、とうとう行かせてもらえることになった。母親は、パンケーキとワインの代わりに、乾いたパンと水を持たせた。ぬけ作が森に入ると、白髪頭の老人が近づき、食べ物と飲み物をわけてほしいと頼んだ。

The Golden Goose

Dunderhead replied, "Sit down my good fellow, I only have bread and water, but you are welcome to share that with me." When he tasted his food, Dunderhead found that his dry bread had turned into a lovely cake and the water had become wine.

After they had shared the meal, the old man said, "Because you have a kind heart and have shared your meal with me, I will do you a good turn. Over there stands an old tree; cut it down, and you will find something worth having in the trunk."

Dunderhead cut the tree down, and as it hit the ground a golden goose fell out. He picked it up and went into town and took a room for the night.

The landlord of the house where he was staying had three daughters. As soon as they saw the wonderful goose they wanted to have it. When Dunderhead left his room, the eldest daughter went quietly in and picked up the goose. Straight away she realized something was wrong as she could not get her hands free. She called out to her sisters that she was stuck fast and they rushed in to help her. Before long they too were sticking to the goose and ended up having to pass the night with it.

■my good fellow ねえ君《呼びかけ》 ■do ~ a good turn ~に良い結果をもたらす ■landlord 图(宿などの)主人 ■straight away すぐに ■stick to ~にくっつく

金のガチョウ

　ぬけ作は答えた。「ねえ、おじいさん、座ってよ。パンと水しかないけれど、いっしょに食べよう」。ぬけ作が食べようとすると、乾いたパンはおいしいパンケーキに、水はワインになっていた。

　食事をわけ合ったあと、老人が言った。「あんたは心がやさしくて、わしに食べ物をわけてくれた。だから、お返しをしよう。向こうに古い木が立っているから、切ってごらん。そうすれば、幹のなかにいい物が見つかるよ」

　ぬけ作はその木を切り落とした。木が地面に倒れると、金のガチョウが落ちてきた。ぬけ作はそれを抱えて町に行き、その夜は部屋を取って泊ることにした。
　ぬけ作が泊った宿屋の主人には、娘が3人いた。娘たちはすばらしいガチョウを目にするやいなや、ほしいと思った。ぬけ作が部屋を出ると、長女が部屋に忍び込み、ガチョウを持ち上げた。その途端、何かおかしいと感じた。手を離せなくなったのだ。長女が妹たちに、ガチョウにぴったりくっついてしまったと叫ぶと、急いで助けに来た。やがて妹たちもガチョウにぴったりくっつき、そのまま一晩過ごすことになった。

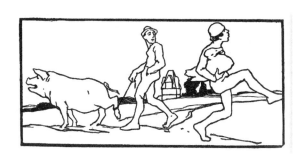

The Golden Goose

The next morning, Dunderhead took his goose and left, saying nothing to the three girls sticking to it. They were forced to run along behind him. In the middle of the field they passed a well-known churchman and when he saw the group he shouted at the girls, "What are you doing running after a man like that? It's not right, wait till I tell your father." When the girls continued running behind Dunderhead and the goose, he ran after them and caught hold of the youngest. Straight away he was caught fast, unable to free himself and found himself having to run along behind the girls.

A little way along the road they passed a friend of the churchman, a very important member of the town government. When he saw his friend running after the girls, he said, "What are you doing? Think of what this looks like. A man of your age and position running after three young girls."

■churchman 图牧師 ■wait till 〜したら驚くよ ■catch hold of 〜をつかむ
■straight away すぐに ■think of 〜について考える

金のガチョウ

　次の朝、ぬけ作はガチョウを抱いて宿屋を出たが、くっついた3人の娘のことなど気にもしなかった。娘たちはぬけ作のあとを走らざるを得なかった。野原のまんなかで、一行はみんながよく知っている牧師を追い越した。牧師は一行を見ると、娘たちに叫んだ。「あんな男のうしろを追いかけるなんてどういうことだ？　そんなことをしてはいけないよ。あんたたちの父親に言ったらびっくりするよ」。それでも娘たちがぬけ作とガチョウのあとを走り続けると、牧師はあとを追いかけ、末の娘をつかんだ。その途端、牧師は末の娘にぴったりくっついて離れられなくなり、娘たちのうしろを走るはめになった。

　道に沿って少し行くと、一行は牧師の友人を追い越した。その人は町役場の偉い役人だった。役人は友人が娘たちのあとを追っているのを見て言った。「何をしているのだね？　世間体を考えたまえ。あんたのような年で地位のある者が、3人の若い娘たちを追いかけるとはね」

The Golden Goose

As they passed by, he tried to pull the churchman off but he, too, was soon being pulled through the town behind Dunderhead and the goose. As they went along, they passed two workmen and the churchman shouted at them to set them free, but no sooner had the workmen touched one of the group than they too became stuck fast and had to follow where Dunderhead led.

They then came to a town where a king lived. This king had a daughter who was so unhappy that she never laughed. The king had made it known that whoever succeeded in making her laugh could marry her.

Dunderhead took his group past her. As soon as she saw everybody sticking to each other, running behind the goose, she started laughing. As he had made the unhappy princess laugh for the first time, Dunderhead asked for her hand in marriage. The king, however, did not really want Dunderhead as a son-in-law and quickly added another condition to be fulfilled before he could marry her. This time Dunderhead must find a man who could drink twelve bottles of wine at one sitting.

■pass by ～を通り過ぎる　■pull ～ off ～を引き離す　■no sooner ～ than ～するやいなや　■son-in-law 图娘婿　■condition 图条件　■at one sitting 一気に

金のガチョウ

　一行が役人のそばを通ると、牧師を引き離そうとした。ところが役人も、すぐに町じゅうをぬけ作とガチョウのあとを引き回されることになった。一行が進むと、2人の農夫を追い越した。すると牧師は2人に離してくれと叫んだ。ところが農夫たちが一行のひとりに触れるやいなや、ぴったりとくっついてしまい、ぬけ作のあとをついていくはめになった。

　そのうち、一行は王様の住む町に着いた。王様には娘がひとりいたが、いつも不機嫌で、笑ったことがなかった。王様は、だれであれ娘を笑わせることができれば、その者を娘と結婚させる、というおふれを出していた。

　ぬけ作は一行を連れて姫の前を通った。だれもが互いにくっついて、ガチョウのあとを走っているのを見るやいなや、姫は笑い出した。ぬけ作は不機嫌な姫をはじめて笑わせることができたので、姫との結婚を申し入れた。ところが、王様はぬけ作を娘婿にすることをあまり望んでいなかったので、急いで別の条件を出し、姫と結婚したければ、それを満たすように言った。今度は、ワイン12瓶を一気に飲める男を見つけなければならなかった。

The Golden Goose

Dunderhead thought about the gray-haired old man who had helped him before and went back to the forest to look for him. He found the little man sitting under a tree looking very unhappy.

"What's up?" asked Dunderhead.

"Well," replied the old man, "I haven't had a good drink for many days and I am as dry as a bone. I feel like I could drink a whole lake of wine."

"Come with me, my friend," said Dunderhead, "I've got just the thing for you!"

He led him back to the king's palace and to the great surprise of everyone, the gray-haired old man not only drank the twelve bottles but asked for more!

Dunderhead once more asked to marry the daughter but the king set a new condition. This time a man had to be found who could eat a mountain of bread. Once again Dunderhead returned to the forest and found the gray-haired old man sitting under the same tree looking tired and thin.

■what's up? どうしたのですか？　■as dry as a bone 乾き切った　■feel like 〜したい気分である　■just the thing まさにぴったりのもの

金のガチョウ

　ぬけ作は以前助けてくれた白髪頭の老人を思い出し、森に戻って捜した。すると、その小さな老人が木の下に腰かけて、とても悲しそうにしていた。

「どうしたのですか？」ぬけ作がたずねた。
「実はな」老人が答えた。「何日もろくに飲んでいないんだ。まるで骨のように乾き切ってしまったよ。湖一杯分のワインだって飲めそうだよ」

「いっしょに来てくれませんか、おじいさん」ぬけ作が言った。「あなたにぴったりの物がありますから！」
　ぬけ作は老人を王様の宮殿に案内した。だれもがひどく驚いたことに、白髪頭の老人は、12瓶のワインを飲み乾しただけでなく、もっとほしいと言った。
　ぬけ作はもう一度、姫と結婚したいと頼んだが、王様は新たな条件を出した。今度は、山ほどのパンを食べられる男を見つけなければならなかった。またもや、ぬけ作が森に戻ると、白髪頭の老人が同じ木の下に座っていた。老人は疲れてやせこけて見えた。

The Golden Goose

"What's wrong, my friend, you don't look well at all?"

"I have a hunger that I cannot get rid of," replied the old man, "No matter how much I eat, I do not feel full up."

"Maybe I can help," said Dunderhead and led him back to the king's palace.

Although it seemed like all the bread in the kingdom had been brought to the palace, the old man sat down and started eating. Within an hour there was nothing left, and he left the palace asking the bystanders if they had any spare food for a hungry old man.

Even then the king would not agree to the marriage but told Dunderhead that he must bring to the palace a ship that could sail on land as well as water. "If you do this one last thing," said the king, "You shall have my daughter's hand in marriage."

Right away Dunderhead set off for the forest. He found the old man and told him of the king's last condition.

"Because you were so kind to me before, I will help you again," said the gray-haired old man.

■get rid of（好ましくないものから）逃れる　■no matter how どんなに〜であろうとも
■bystander 图見物人　■spare 形余分な　■sail 動航行する

金のガチョウ

「どうしたの、おじいさん？ まったく元気がないですね」
「腹が減ってたまらんのだ」老人が答えた。「どんなに食っても、満腹にならんのじゃ」

「ぼくが助けてあげられるかもしれない」と、ぬけ作は言い、老人を王様の宮殿に連れていった。
国じゅうのパンが宮殿に運び込まれたように見えたが、老人は座り込んで食べはじめた。1時間もしないうちに、残さず食べ切ったので、老人は宮殿を出て、腹を空かせた年寄りのために余分な食べ物がないかと、見物人にたずねた。

そのときになっても、王様は結婚を許さず、ぬけ作に陸と海の両方を走る船を、宮殿に持ってくるように命じた。「最後の条件をかなえることができれば」王様が言った。「娘との結婚を認めよう」

すぐに、ぬけ作は森に出かけた。白髪頭の老人を見つけると、王様の最後の条件を話した。
「あんたは前にわしにとても親切にしてくれたから、また助けてやろう」老人が言った。

The Golden Goose

He quickly built a ship that could sail on both land and sea, and Dunderhead sailed in it to the palace. When the king saw it, he knew he could not put Dunderhead off any longer and agreed to the marriage.

The people of the kingdom had grown to like Dunderhead as he answered the conditions laid down by the king, and they were full of joy when the pair got married. Dunderhead went on to live a long and happy life and succeeded to the throne when the old king died.

■grow to ～するようになる ■lay down 命じる ■full of joy 喜びでいっぱいである

金のガチョウ

　老人は、素早く陸と海を走る船を作り、ぬけ作はそれに乗って宮殿まで行った。王様はそれを見ると、これ以上ぬけ作を待たせるわけにいかないと悟り、結婚を認めた。

　王国の人々もぬけ作のことを好きになっていた。それは王様が出したいくつもの条件を満たしたからだった。それで、ぬけ作と姫が結婚すると、人々はとても喜んだ。ぬけ作は末長く幸せに暮らし、年を取った王様が亡くなると、次の王様になった。

覚えておきたい英語表現

> *What a* man I am, (p. 138, 17行目)
> なんてやつだ、俺は。

　Whatを用いた感嘆文ですね。What a 名詞で「なんと〜だろう」という意味を表す…ということはよくご存知だと思います。What a manで「なんてやつだ」という意味です。「なんて凄いやつだ」の意味でも「なんて酷いやつだ」の意味でも使えます。文脈でどちらの意味なのか読み取ればよいのですが、相手をほめるならWhat a great man!のようにgreatとかgoodをつければ、よりはっきりと相手を賞賛する気持ちが伝わるでしょう。

　学校ではこのような感嘆文は…

> *What an* exciting game it is!　なんて面白い試合だろう！

といった「What a + 形容詞 + 名詞 + 主語 + 動詞」の例文で学ぶことと思います。もちろんこれはこれで大事なのですが、日常会話ではもっと簡単な表現も使いますのでご紹介します。ネイティブ度が上がるこれらの表現をぜひ使いこなしてください。

> *What a* shame!　　　残念だ／なんてこった！
> *What a* view!　　　なんて良い眺めだ！
> *What a* surprise!　　まあ、驚いた！

> A man who can kill seven at a stroke is *more than* a match for two.
> （p. 154, 9行目）
> 一打ちで7人を殺せる男にとって2人を相手にするのは簡単だ。

more thanは「〜以上」という意味です。

> I have been living here *more than* 20 years.
> 私はここに20年以上住んでいます。

この他にも「〜以上のもの」「〜どころではない」「〜して余りある」という意味で、日常会話で多用される表現です。例文をあげておきますのでぜひ慣れて、使いこなして下さい。

【例文】

Don't buy *more than* you need.
必要以上に買ってはいけませんよ。

I was *more than* surprised to see you there.
君にそこで会って驚いたなんてもんじゃなかったよ。

I love you *more than* words can say.
言葉で言い尽くせないほど君のことを愛している。

You have done *more than* enough.
君は十分すぎるほどやったじゃないか。

more thanを紹介したのでless thanも紹介しておきましょう。less than 〜は「〜以下」という意味のほかに、「まったく〜でない」「〜とは程遠い」という意味もあります。

The damage was *less than* we feared.
損害は私たちが心配していたほどはなかった。

He works *less than* his boss expected.
彼は上司が期待したほどには働かない。

They sold things at *less than* the actual value.
彼らは商品をむやみに値下げして売った。

[IBC対訳ライブラリー]
英語で読むグリム名作選

2015年3月1日 第1刷発行

著　者　　グリム兄弟
英語解説　出水田隆文
翻　訳　　宇野葉子
発行者　　浦　晋亮
発行所　　IBCパブリッシング株式会社
　　　　　〒162-0804 東京都新宿区中里町29番3号 菱秀神楽坂ビル9F
　　　　　Tel. 03-3513-4511　Fax. 03-3513-4512
　　　　　www.ibcpub.co.jp
印刷所　　株式会社シナノパブリッシングプレス

© IBC Publishing, Inc. 2015

Printed in Japan

落丁本・乱丁本は、小社宛にお送りください。送料小社負担にてお取り替えいたします。
本書の無断複写（コピー）は著作権法上での例外を除き禁じられています。

ISBN978-4-7946-0329-6